PAPER FRICTION

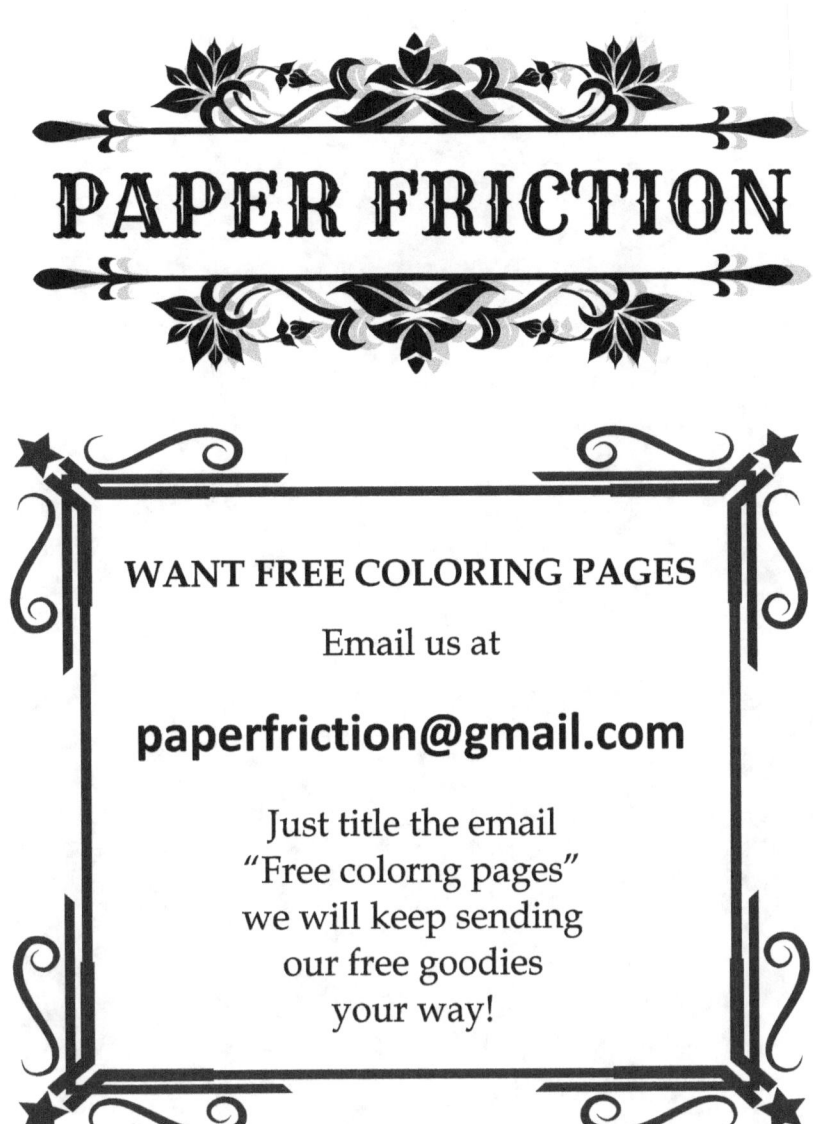

WANT FREE COLORING PAGES

Email us at

paperfriction@gmail.com

Just title the email
"Free colorng pages"
we will keep sending
our free goodies
your way!

Copyright © 2021 by Paper Friction
All rights reserved.

No part of this book may be reproduced or used in any manner
without the prior written permission of the copyright owner,
except for the use of brief quotations in a book review.

You may post colored page on social media if complemented by an artist credit
and the title of the book.

We value our customers and always welcome feedback and suggestions.
If you would like to connect with us please e-mail **paperfriction@gmail.com**
and we will get back to you as soon as possible.

Join our facebook group community for our Contest and Updates.
www.facebook.com/groups/paperfriction/

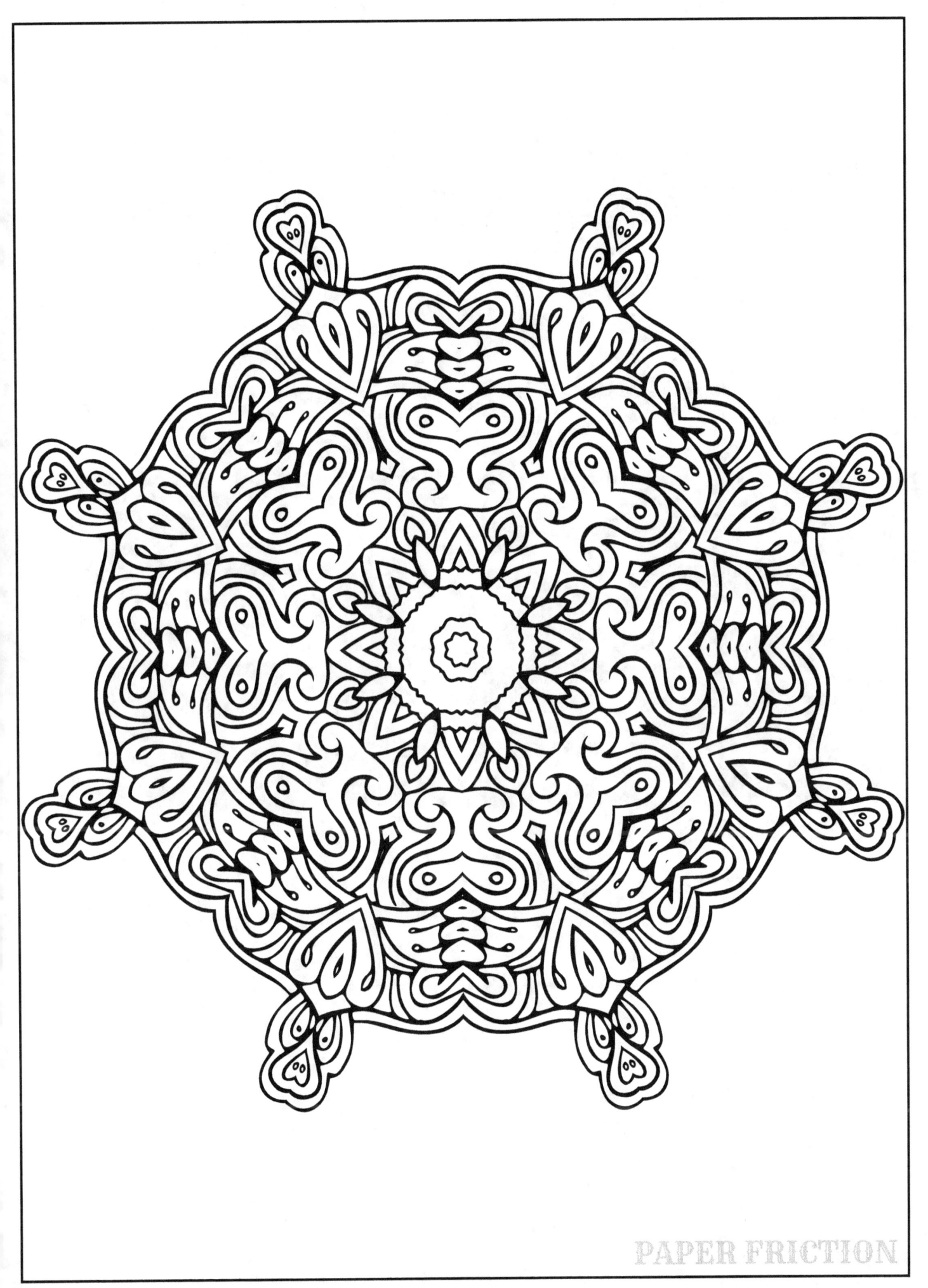

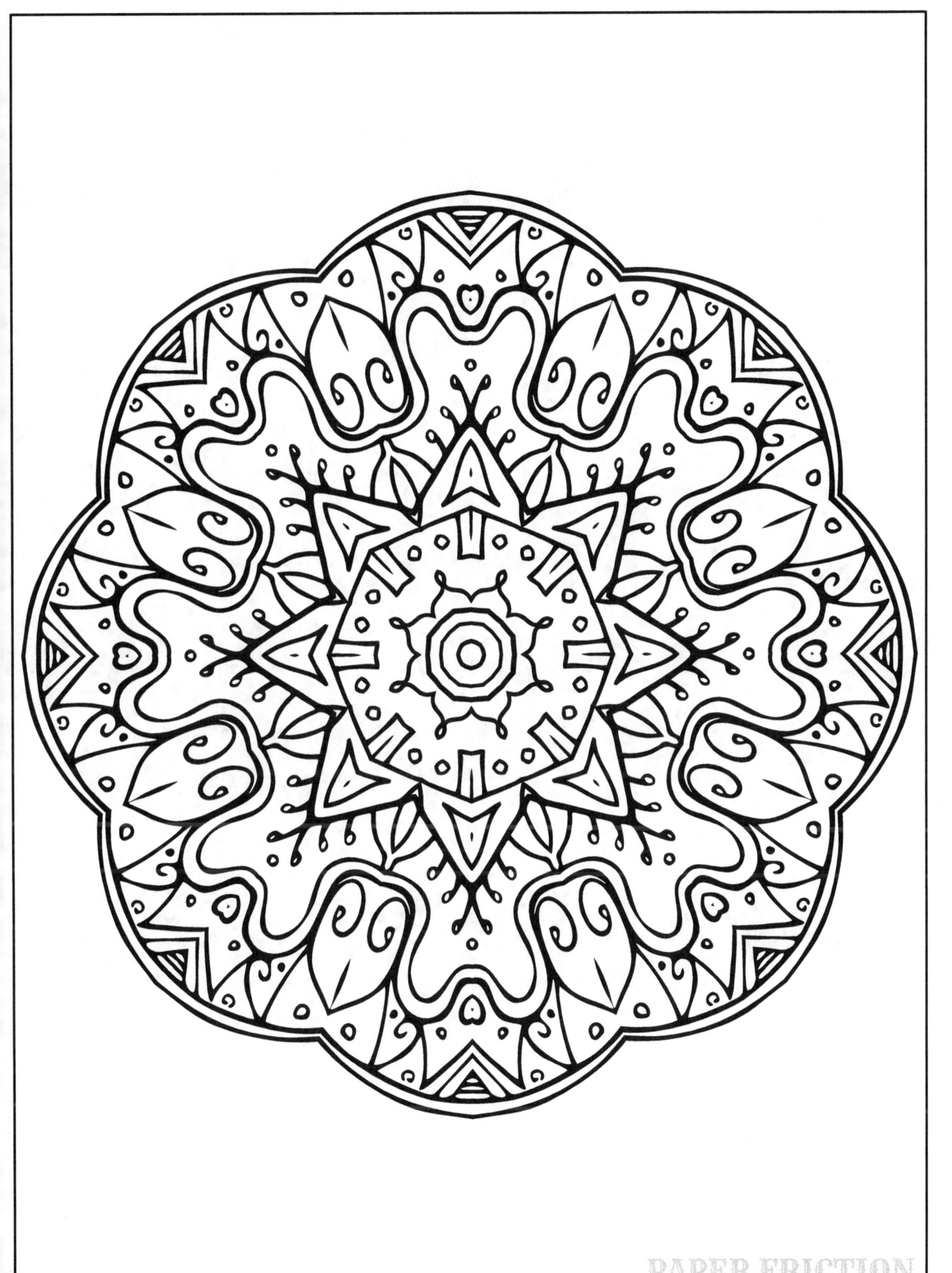

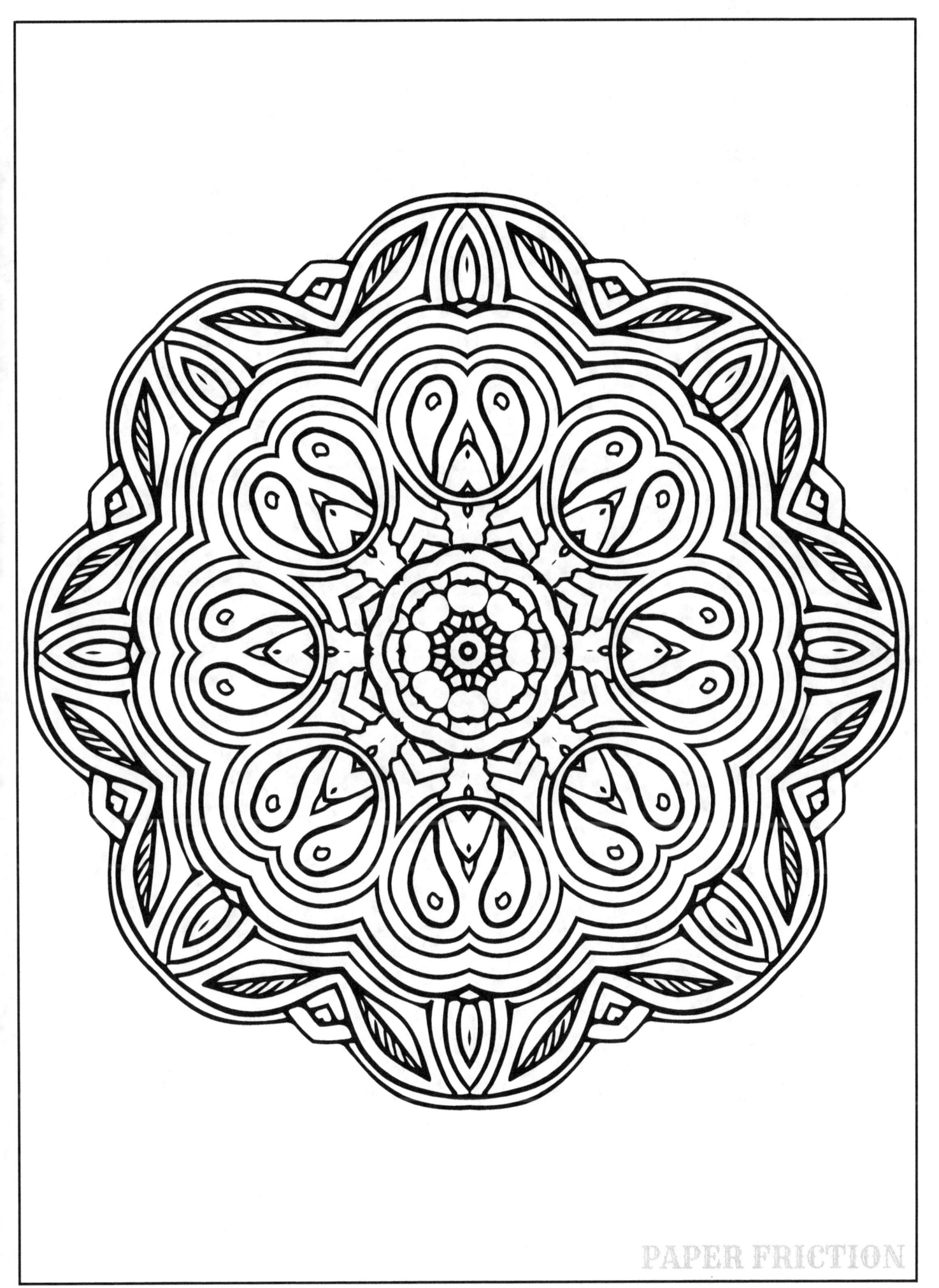

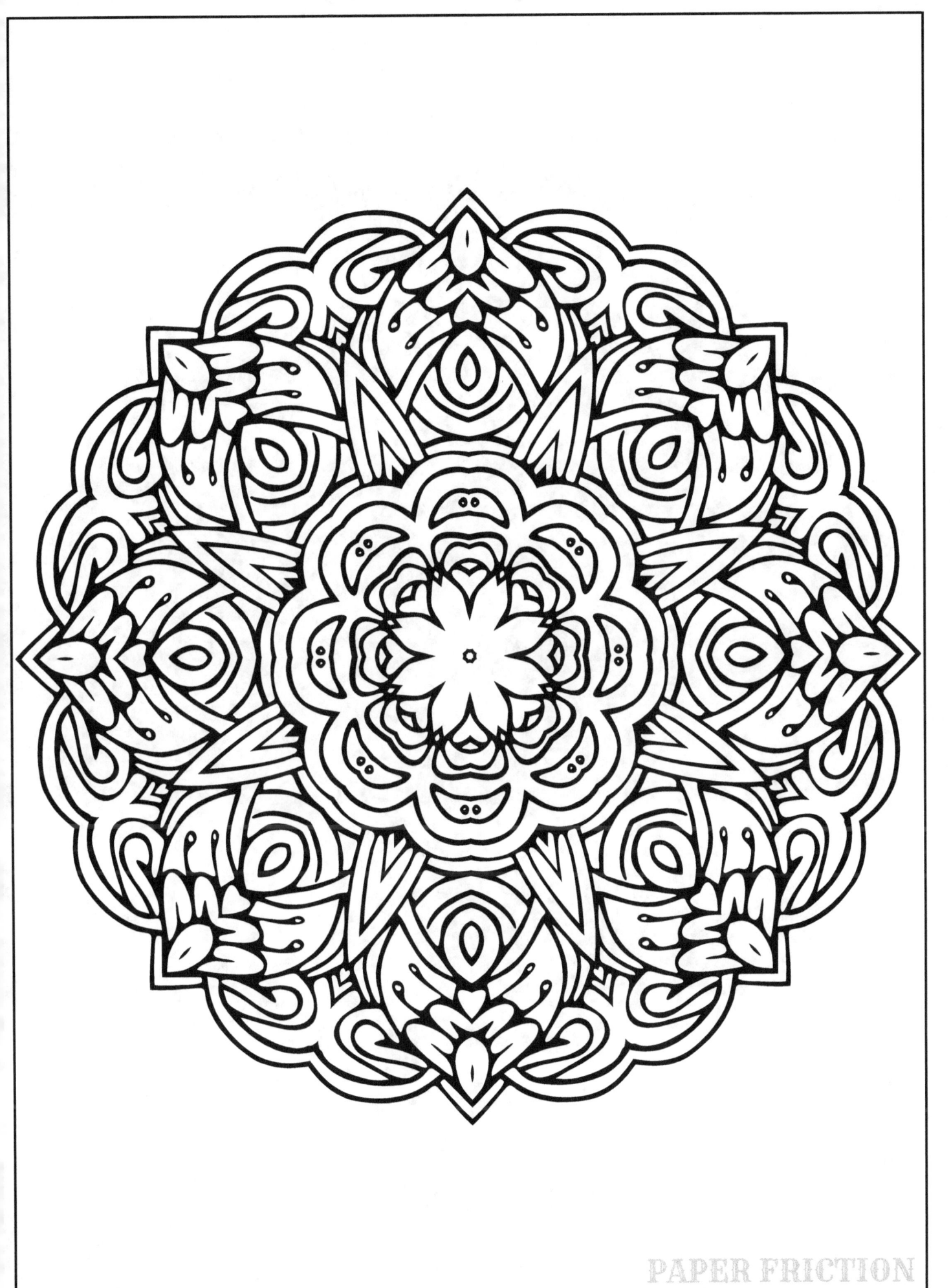

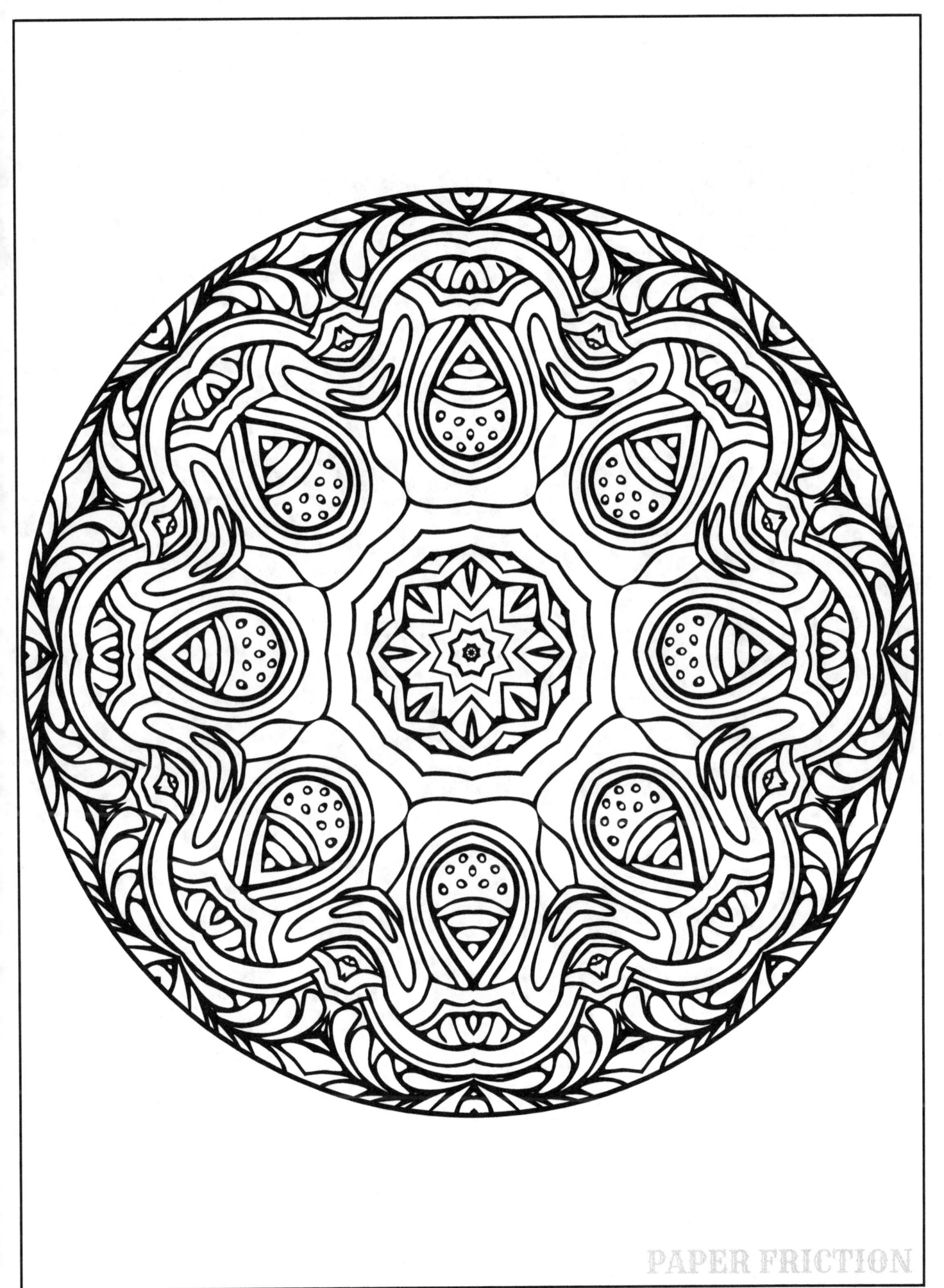

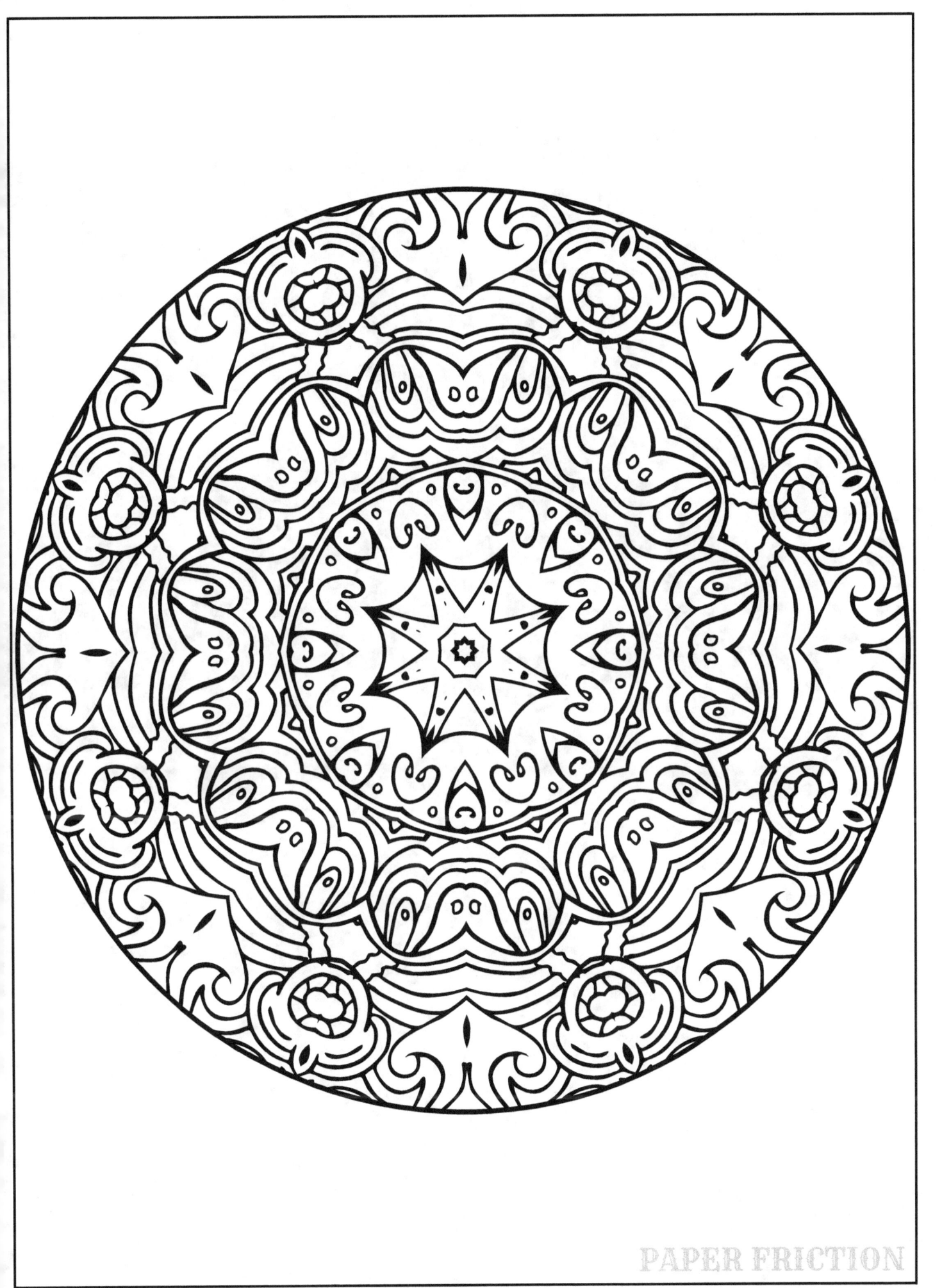

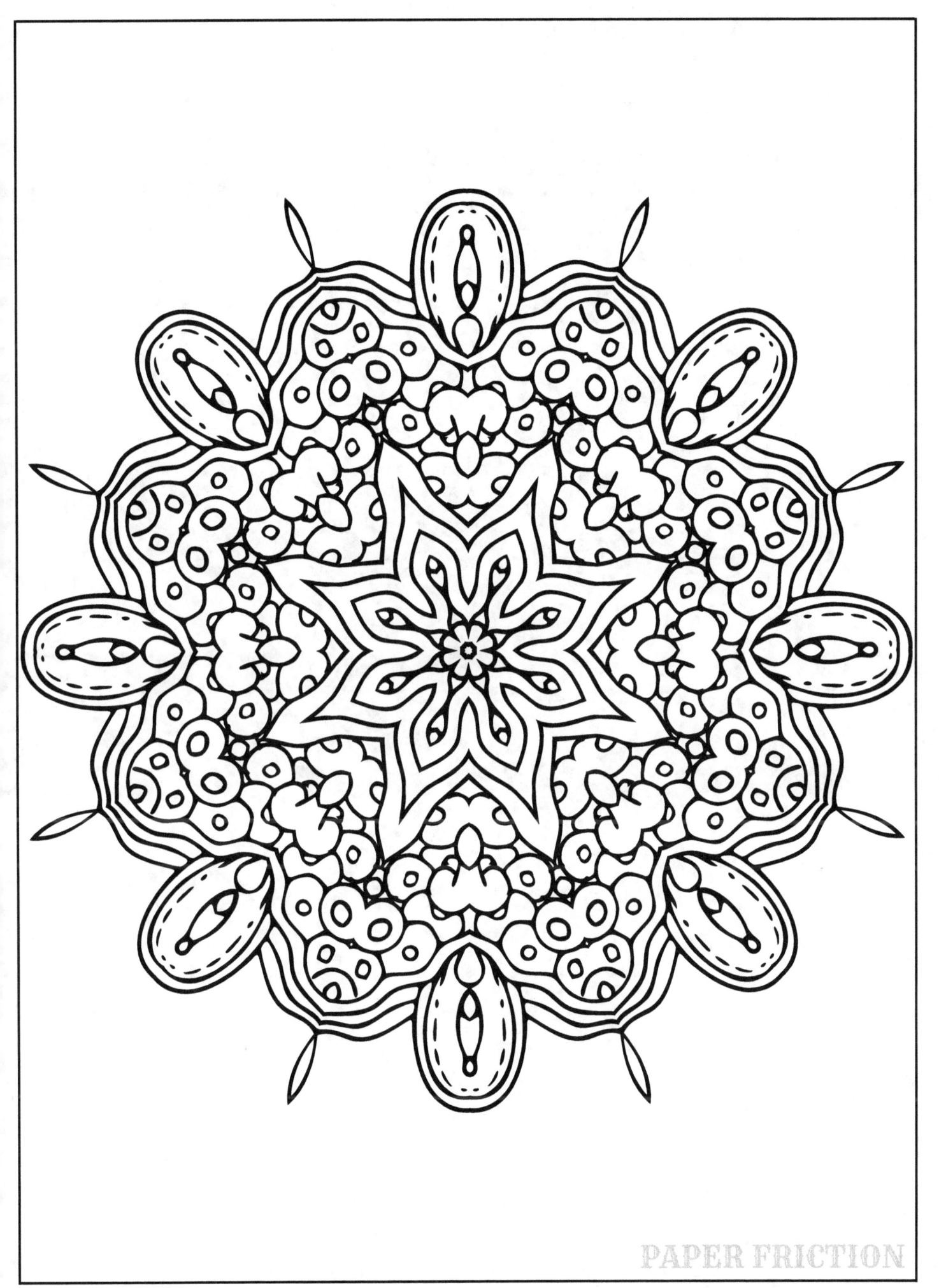

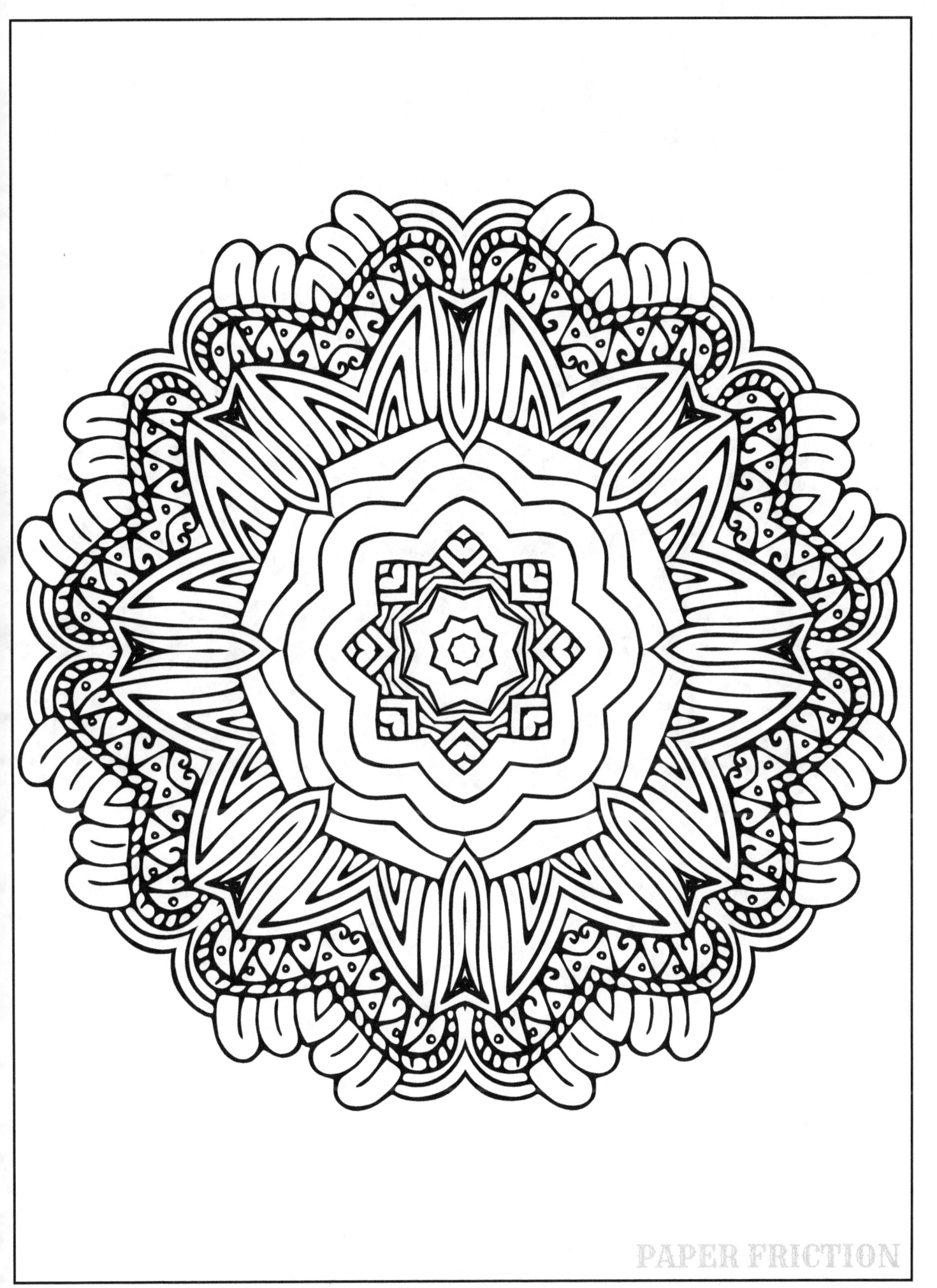

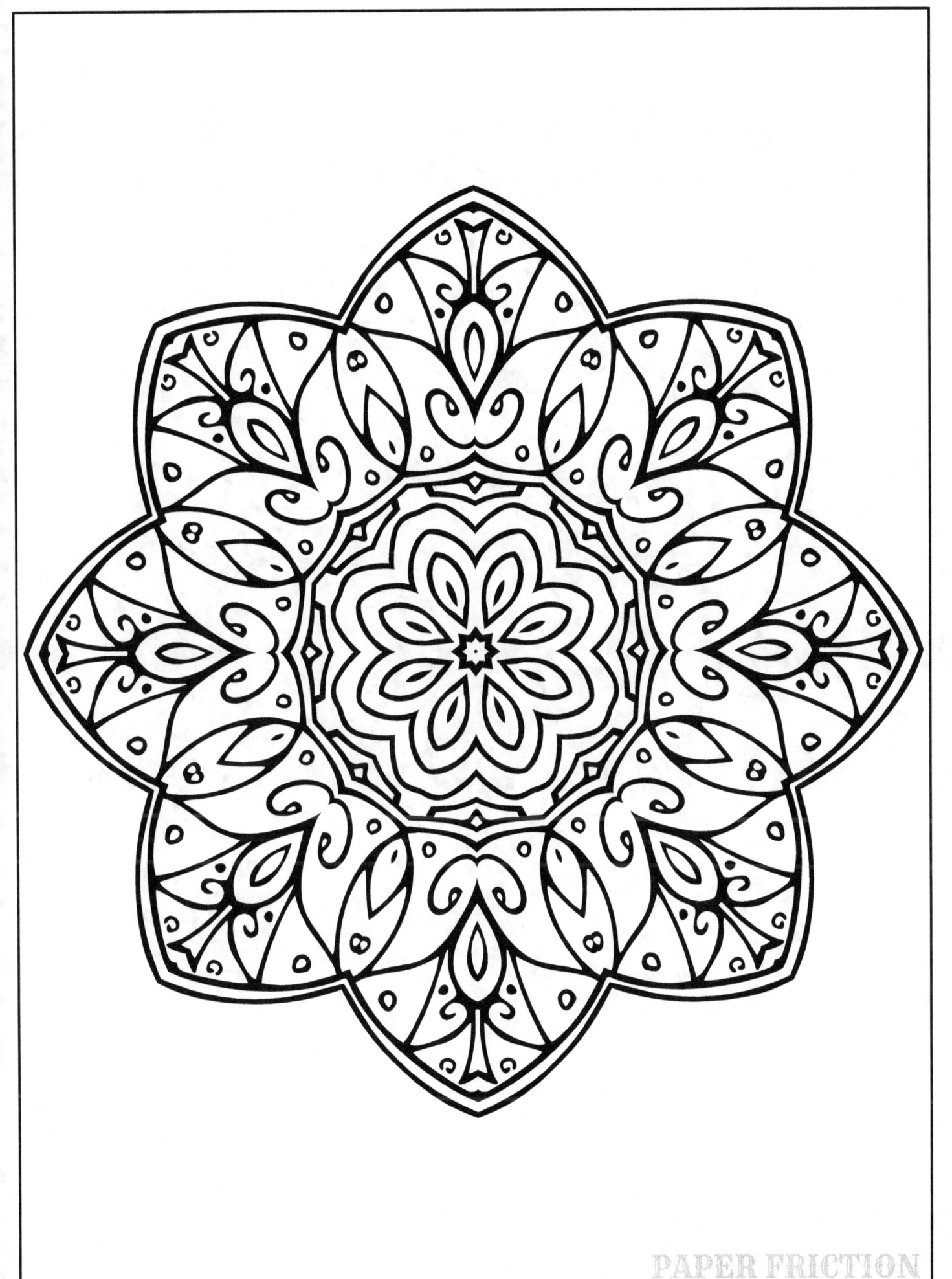

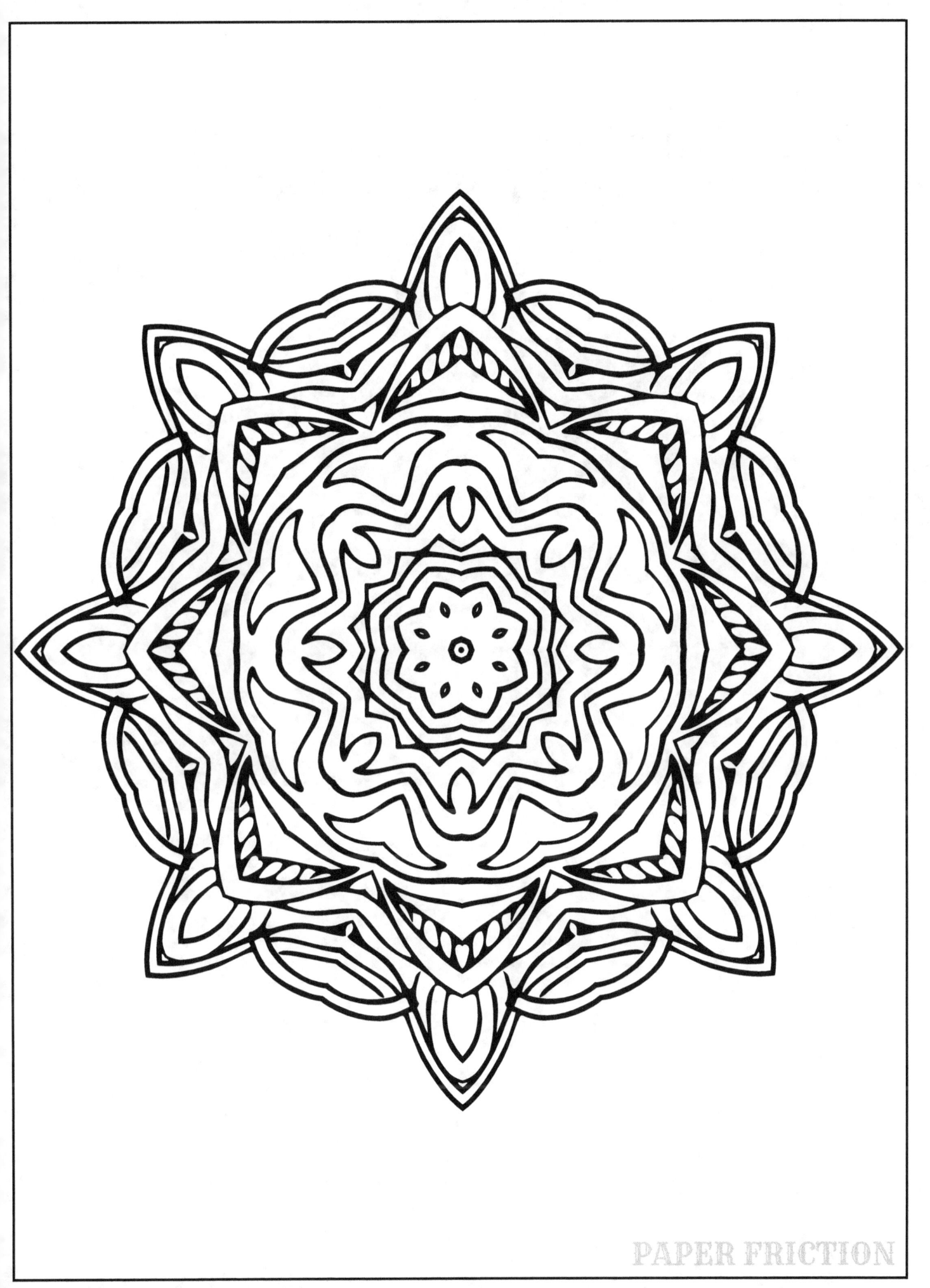

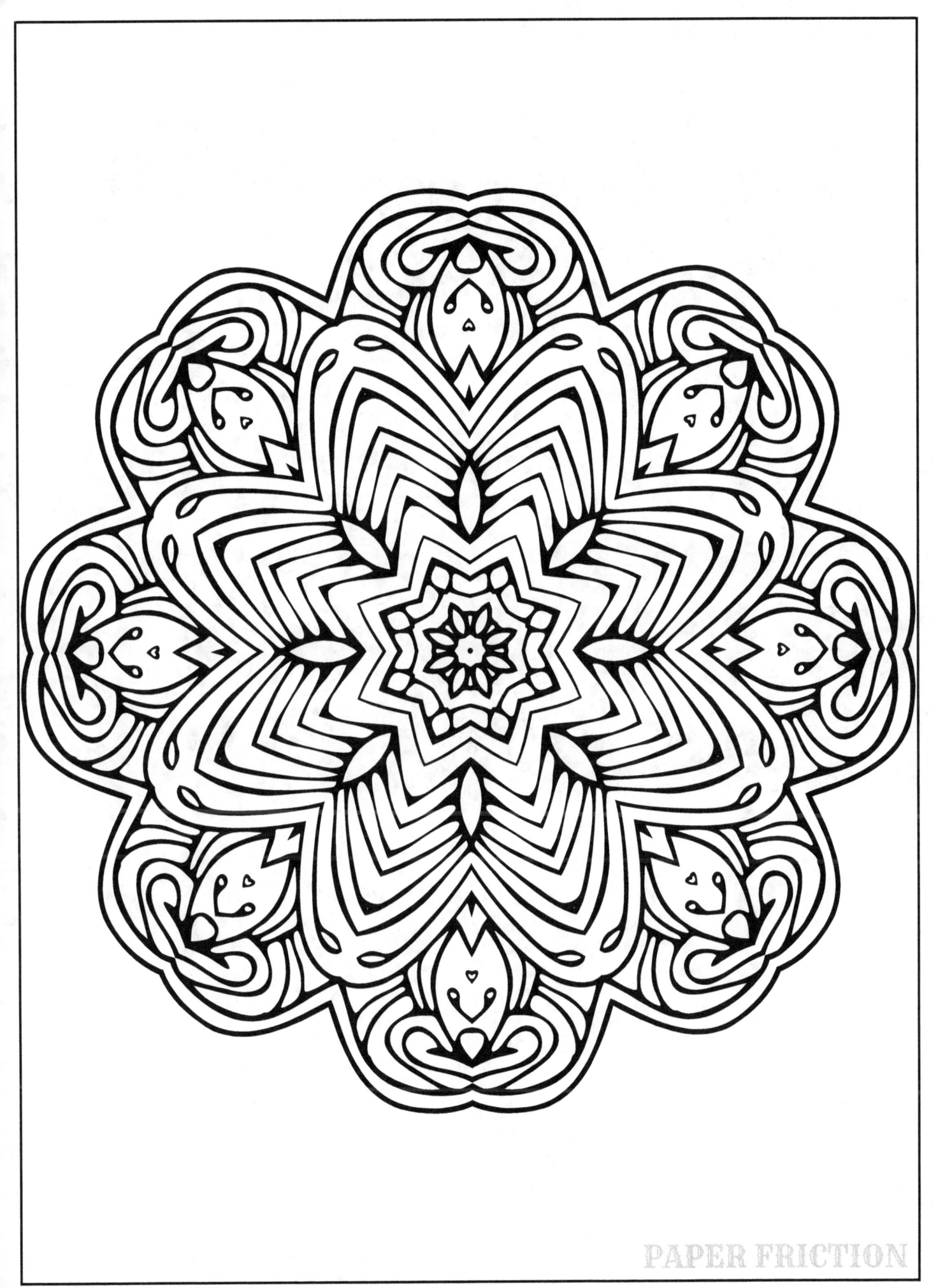

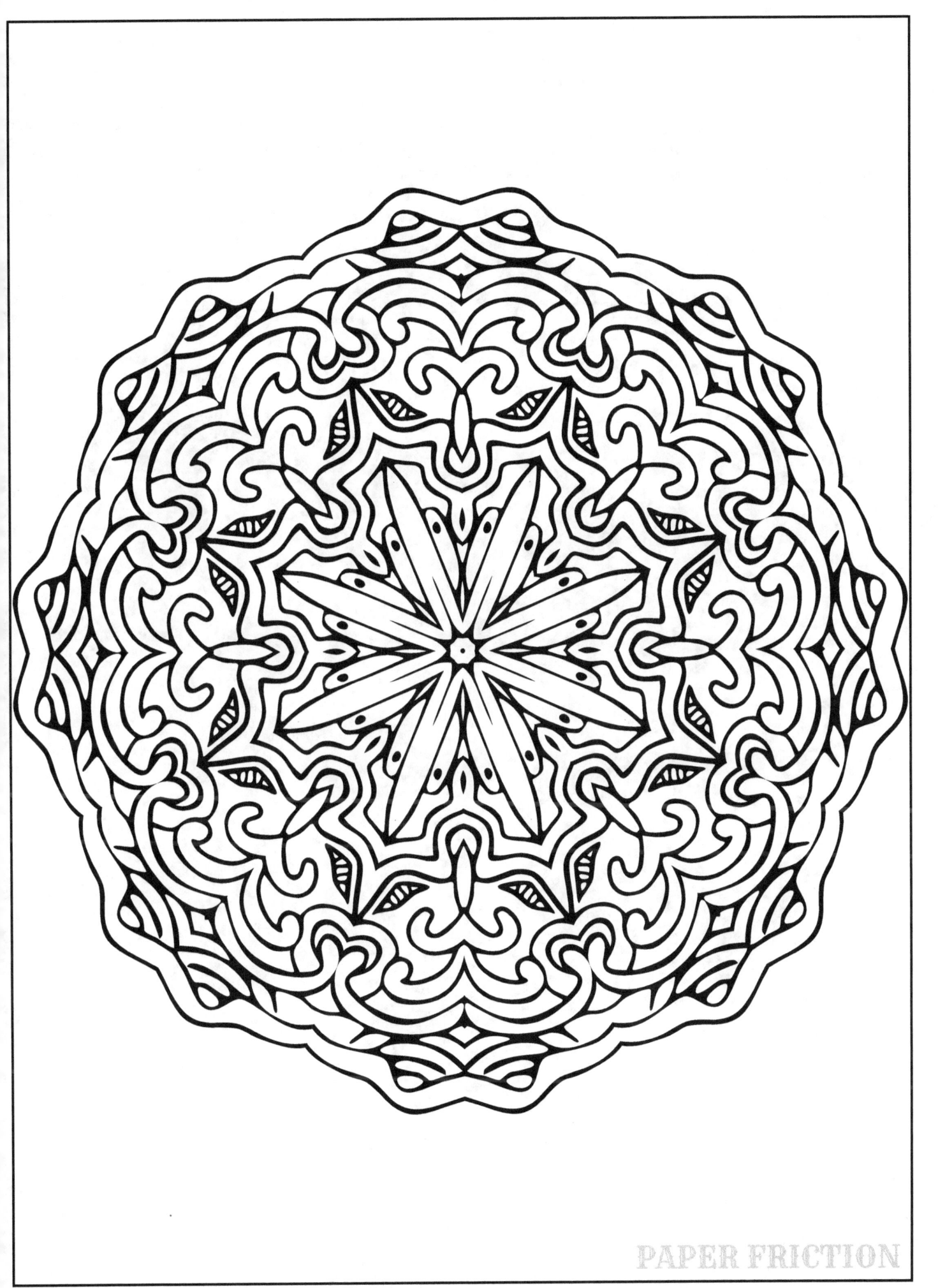

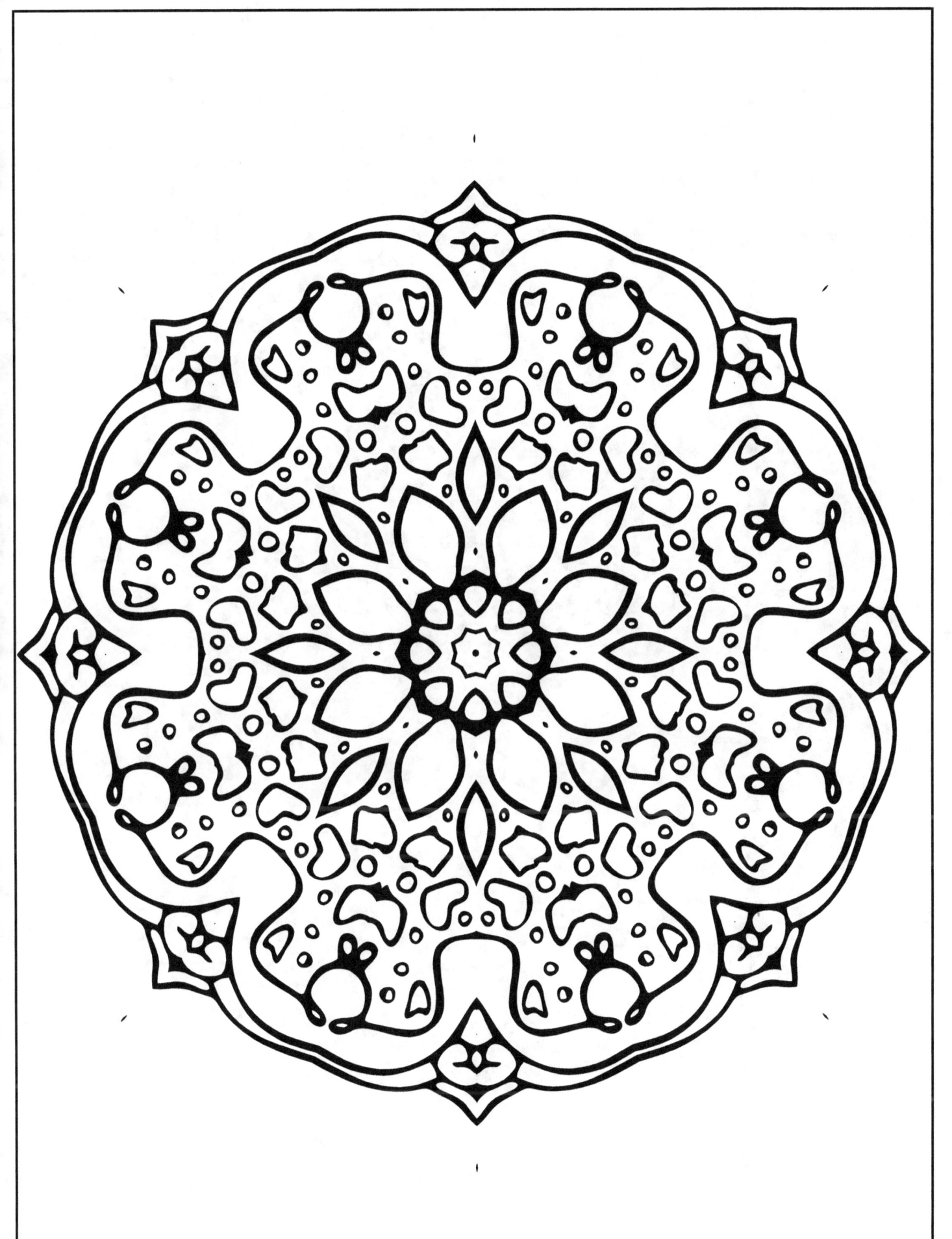

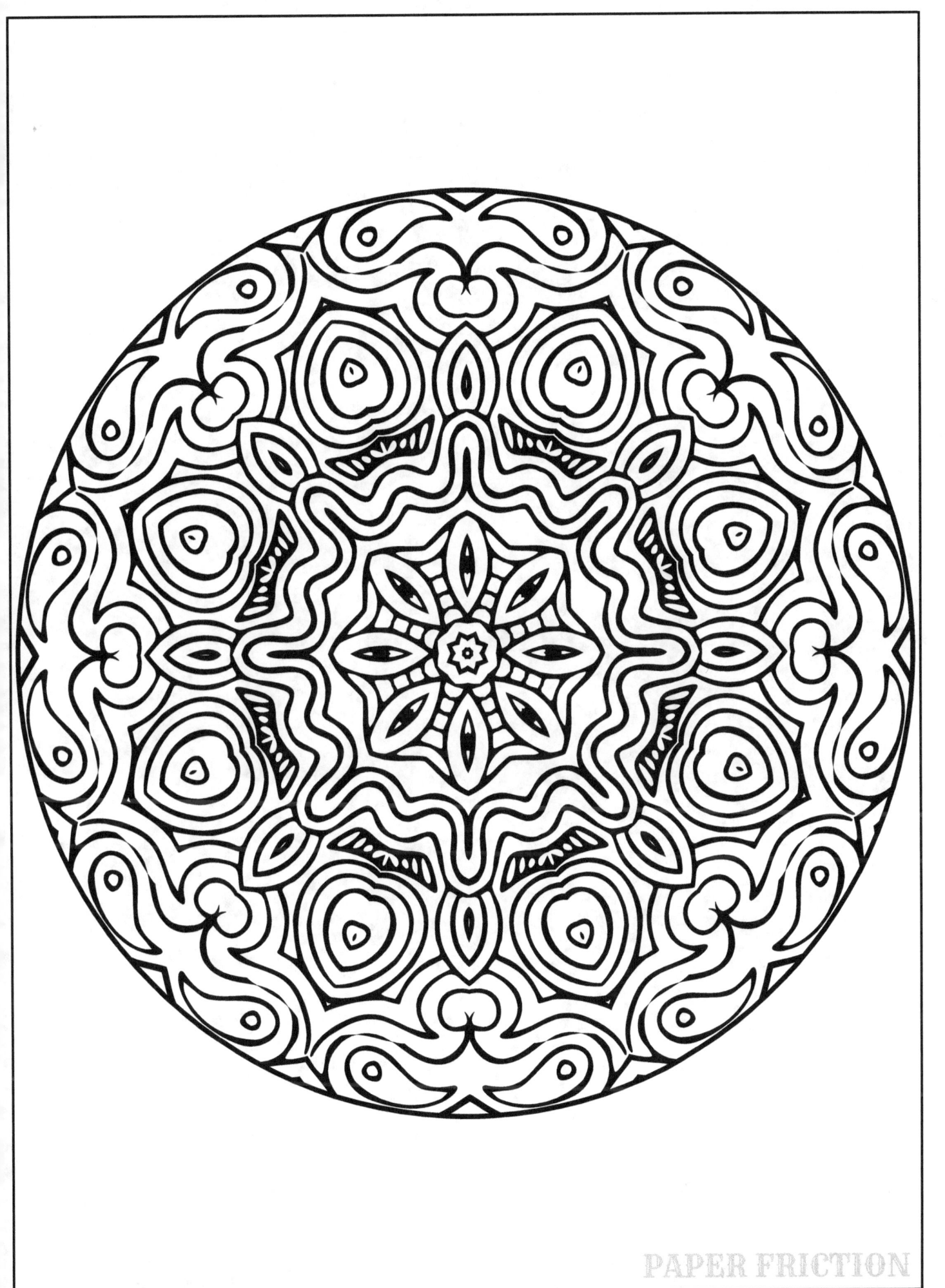

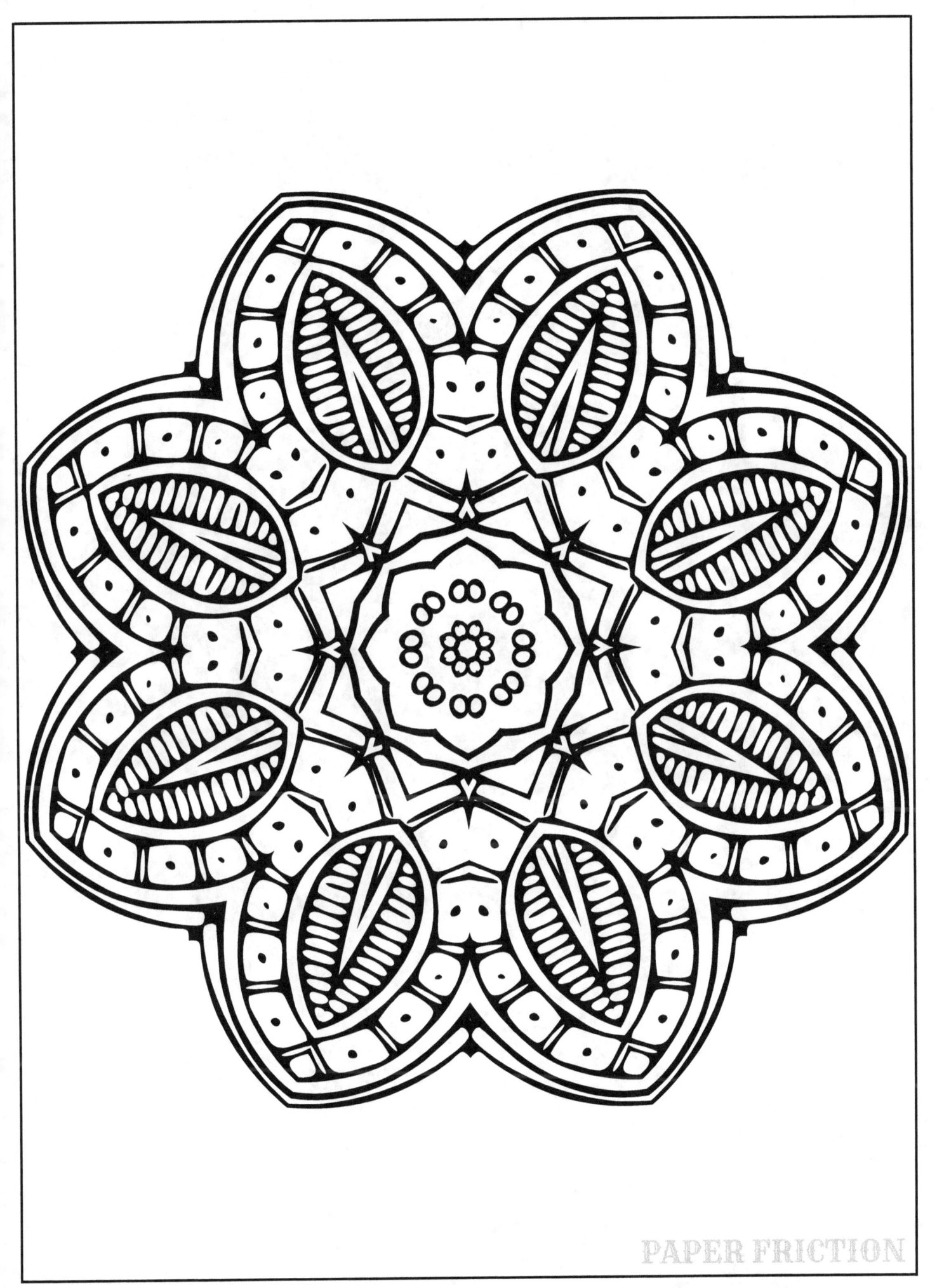

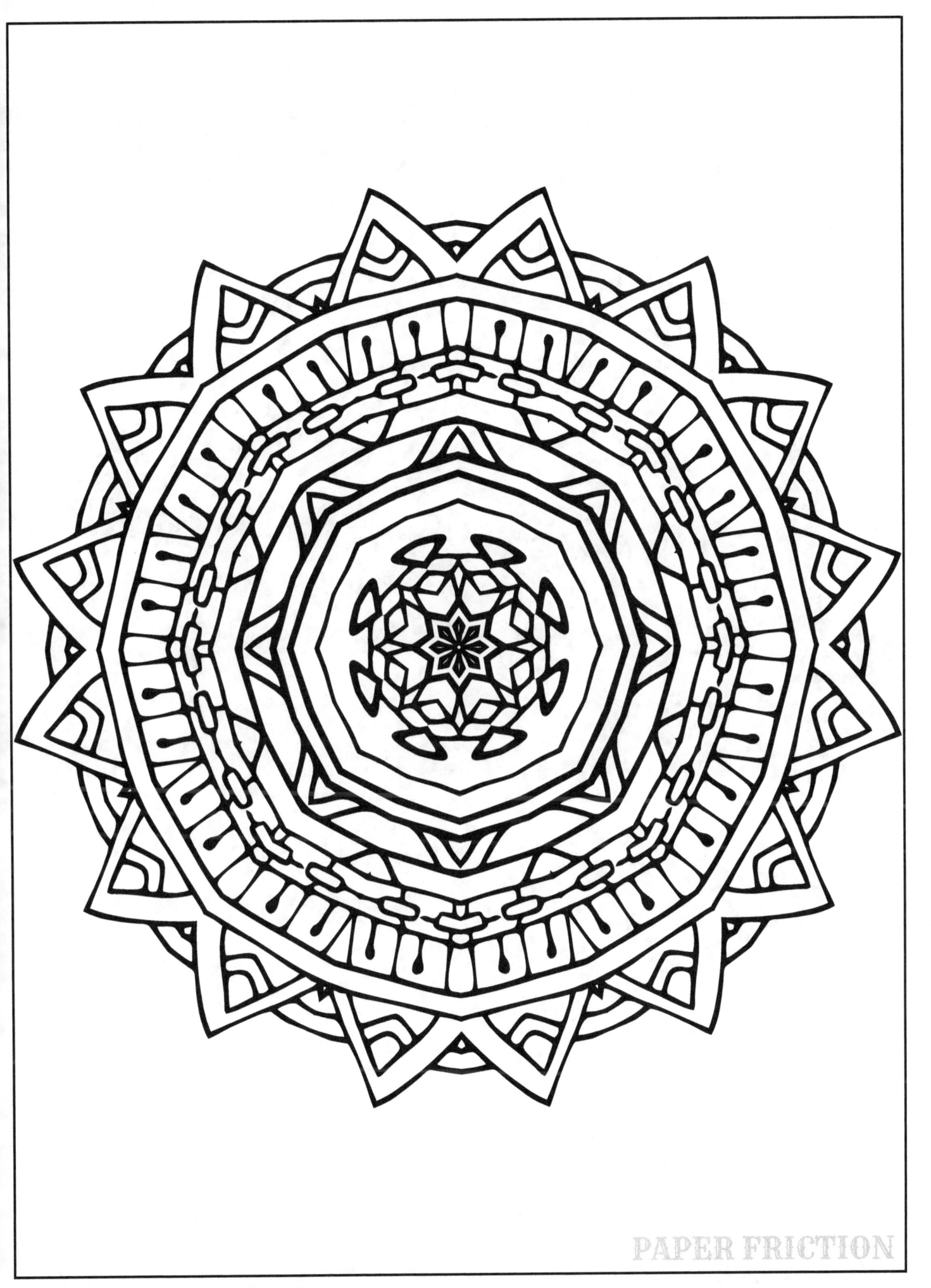

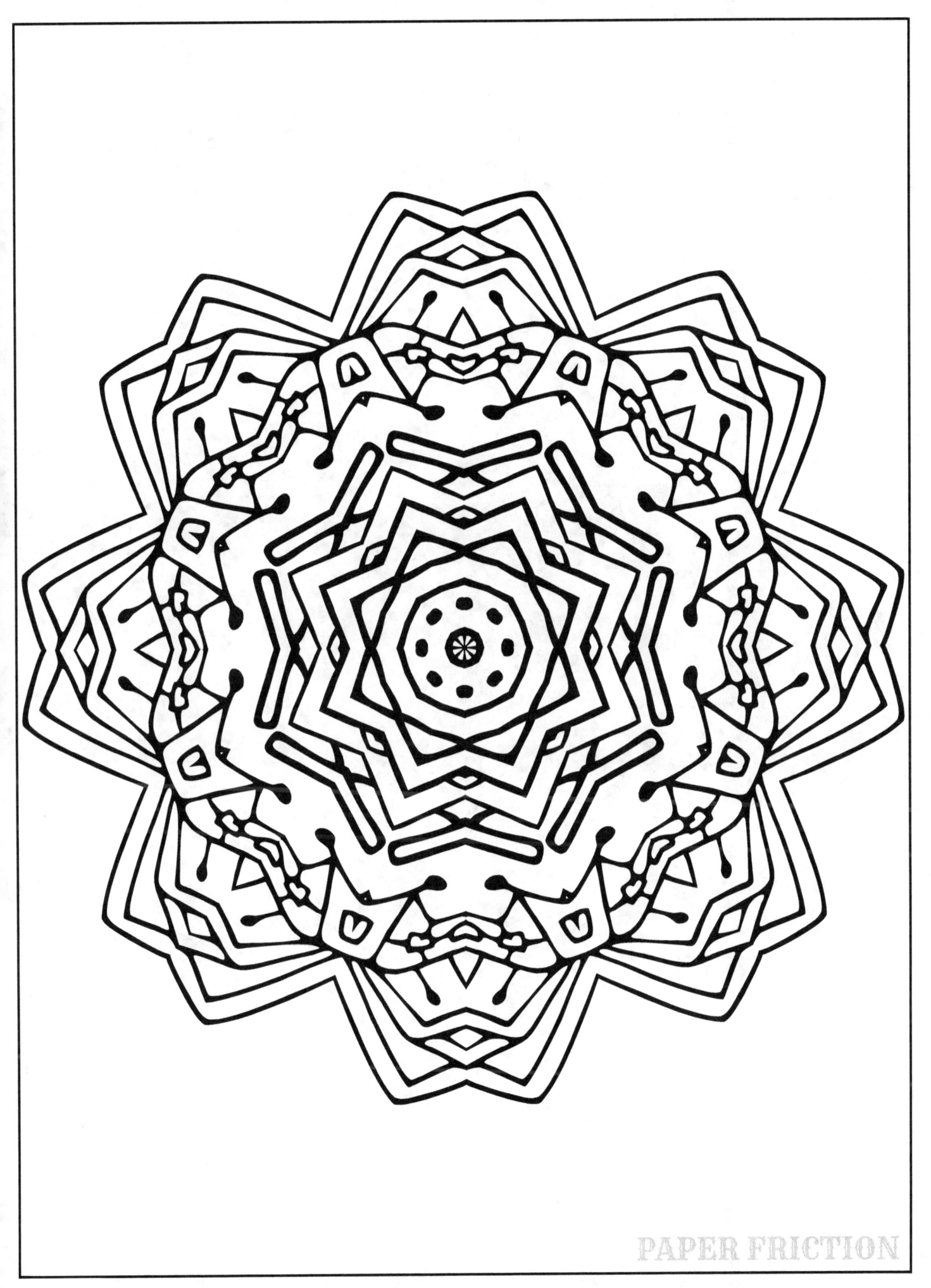

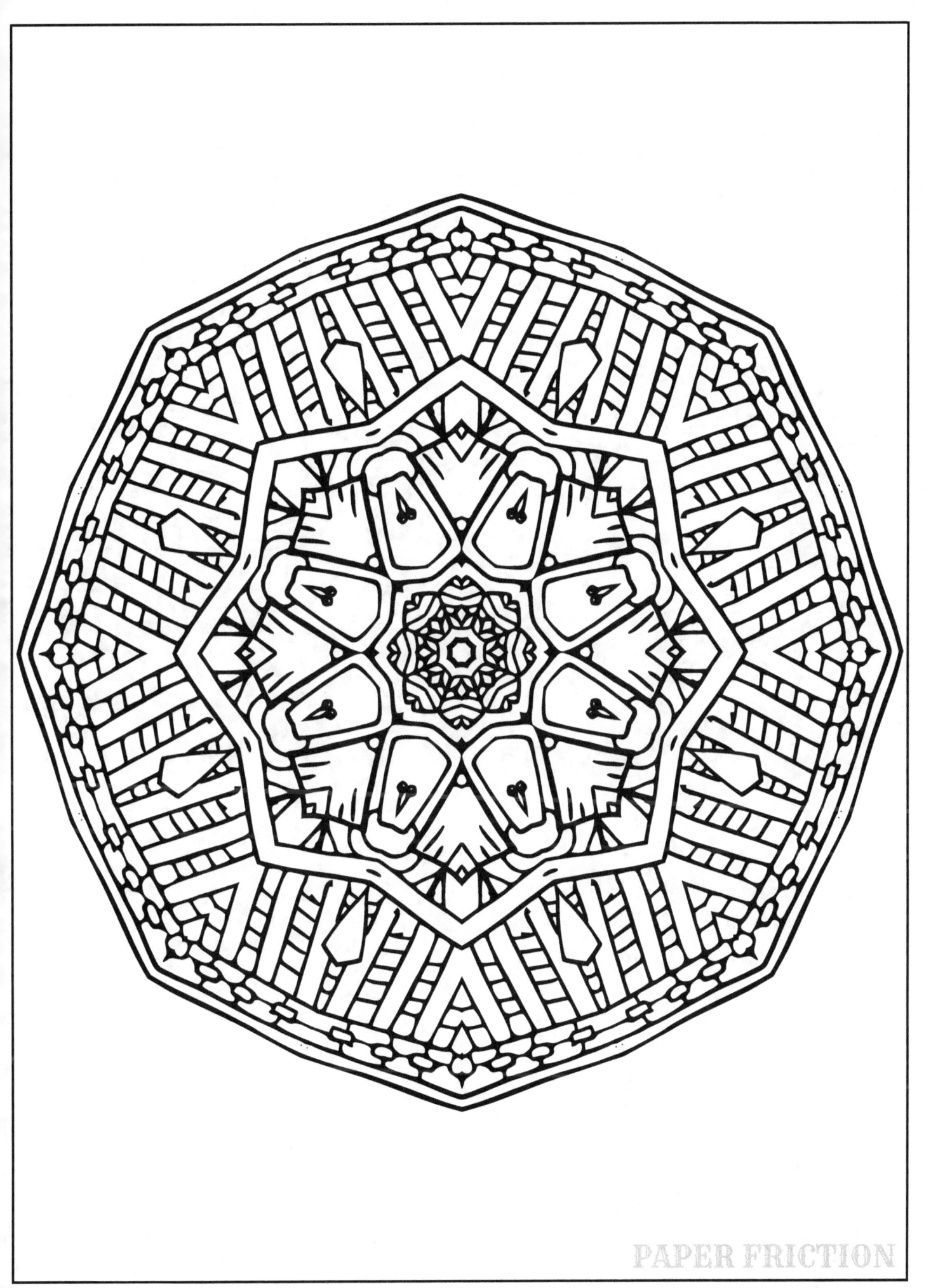

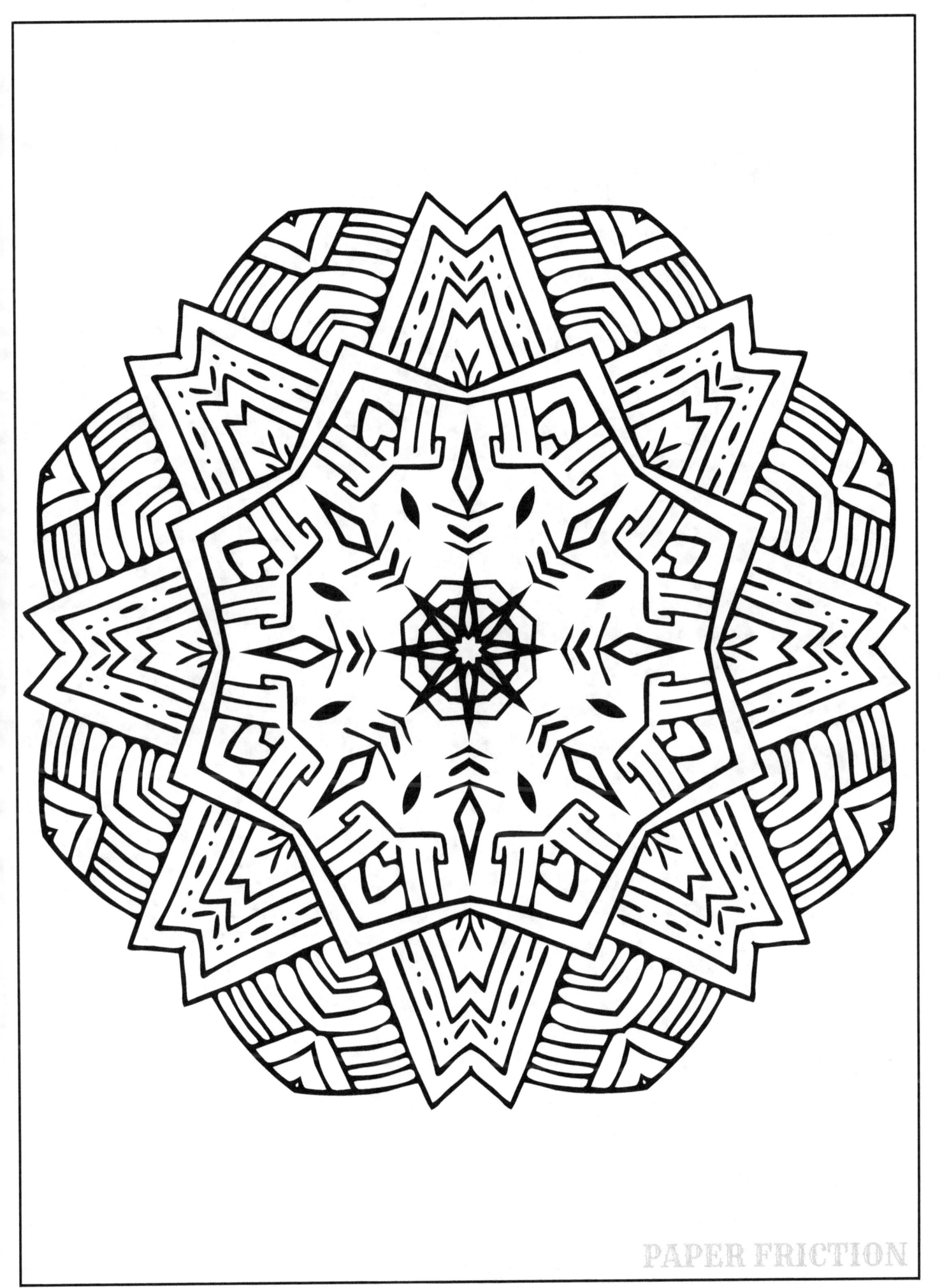

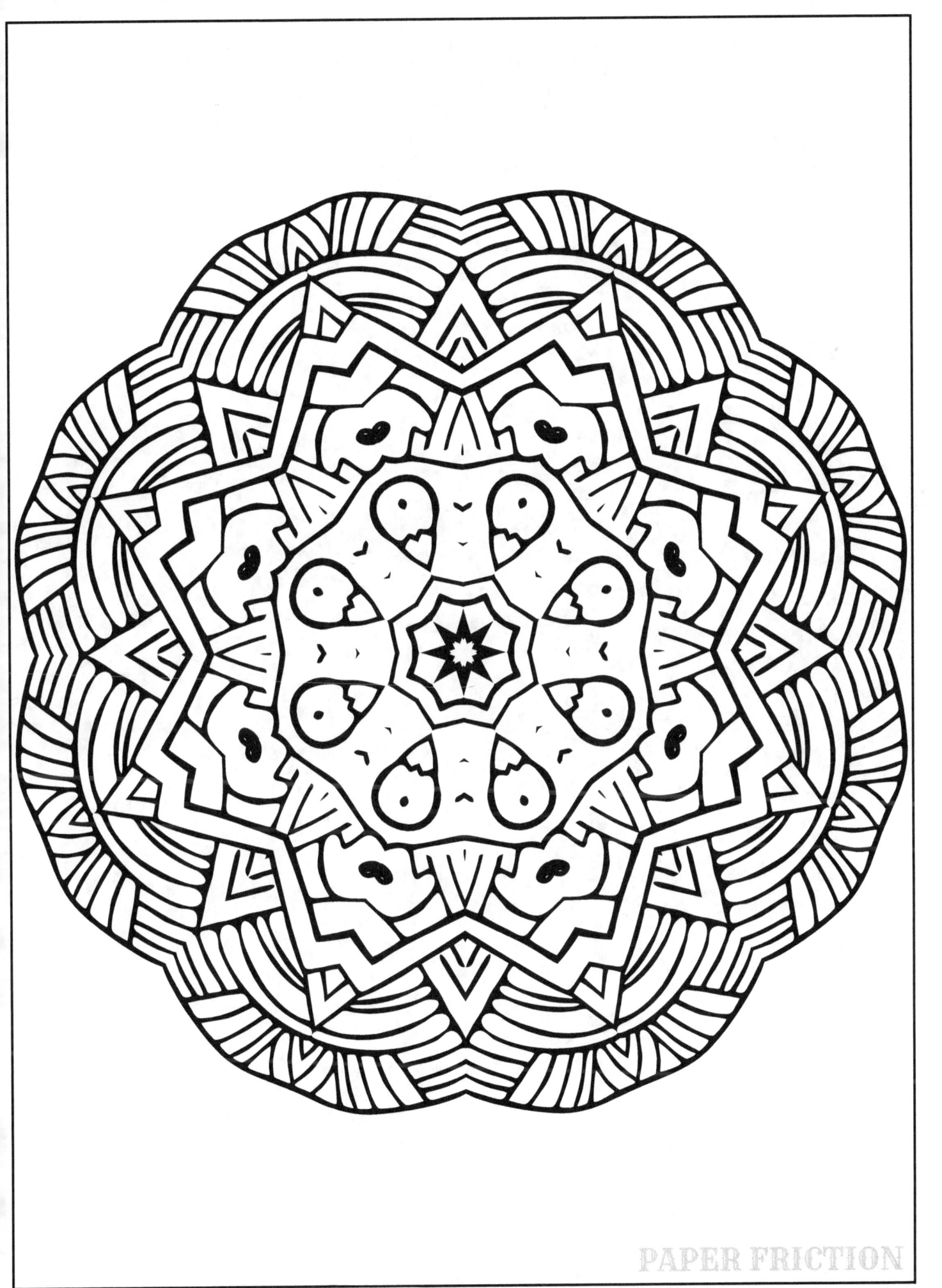

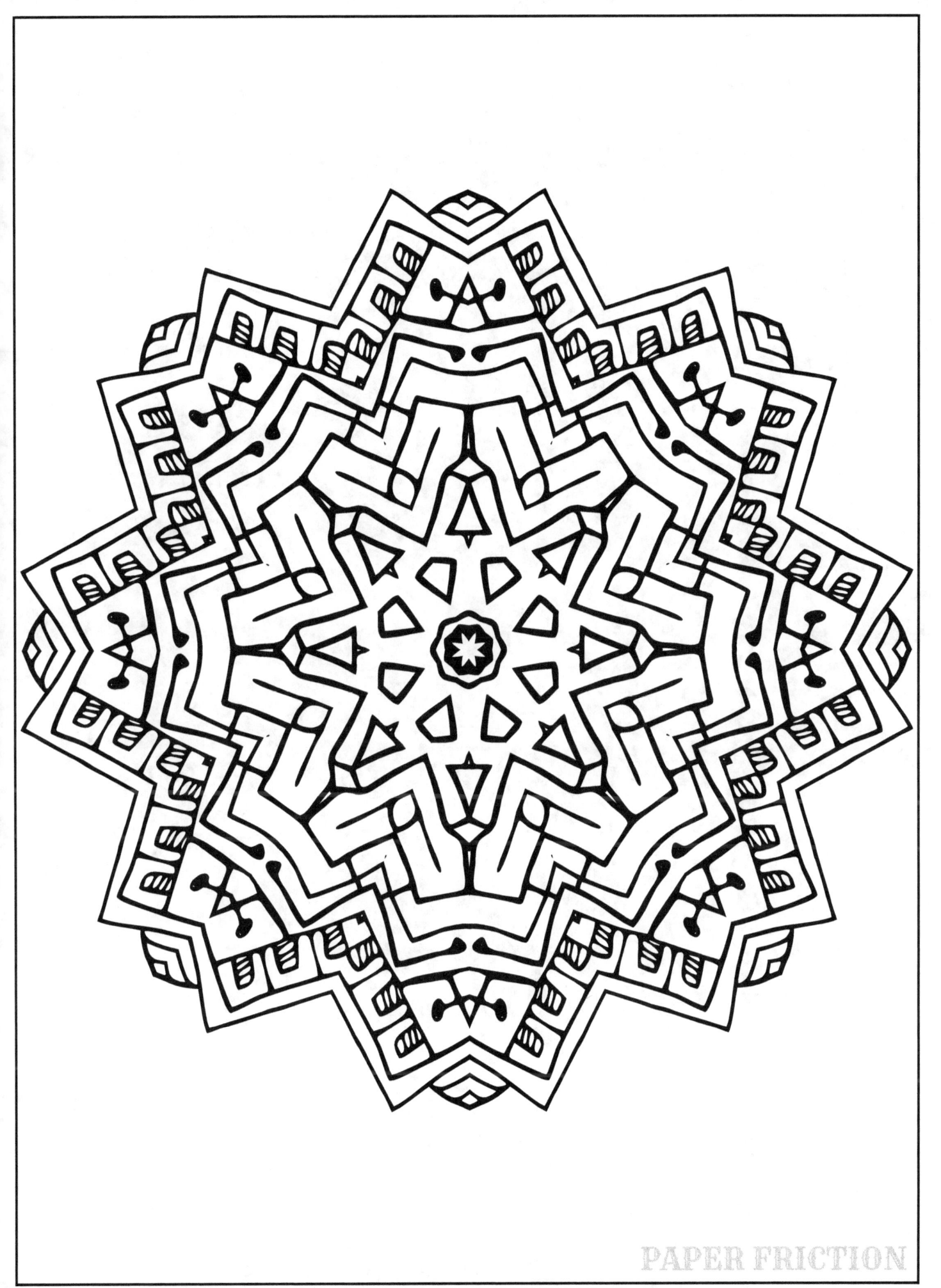

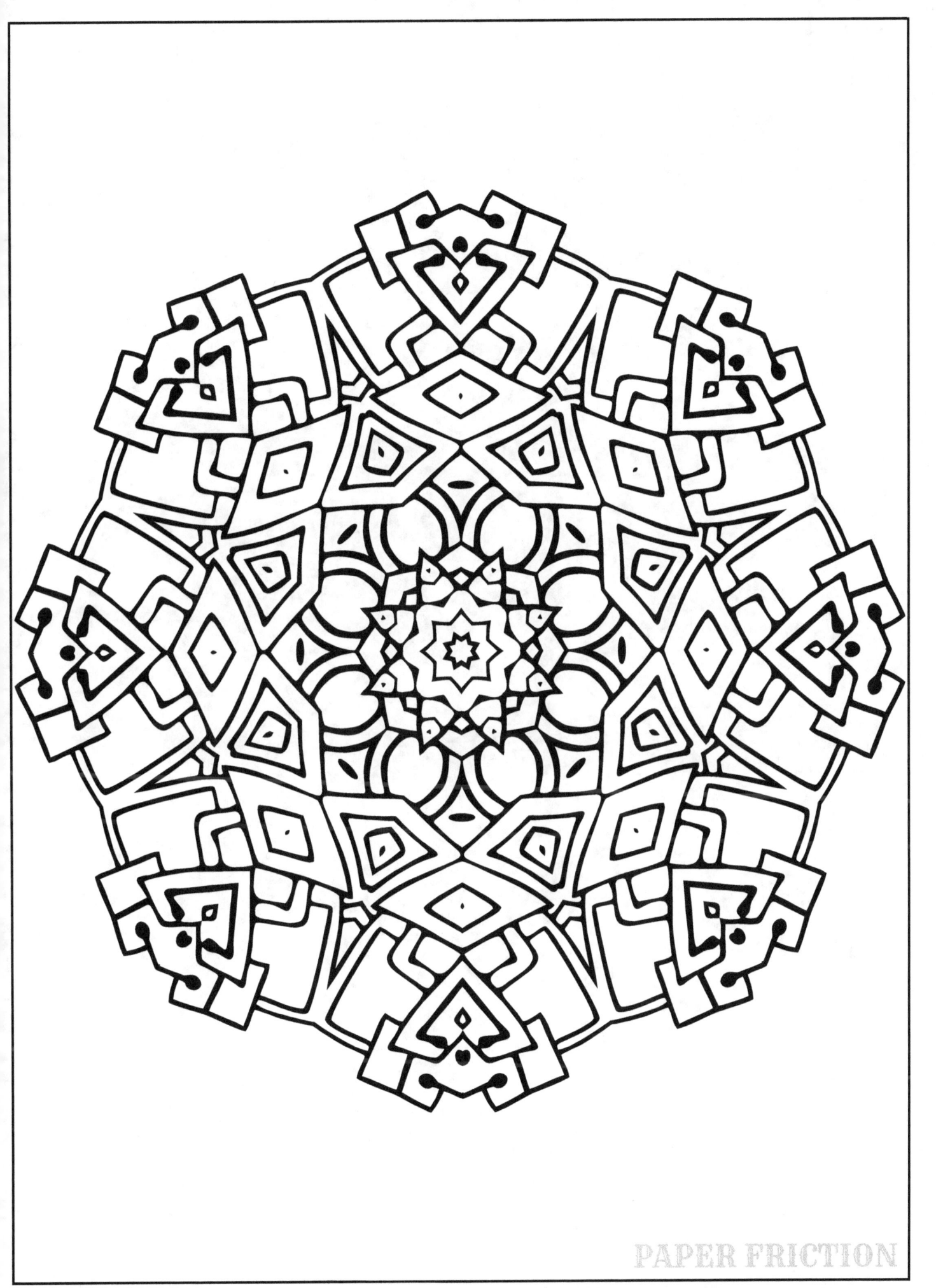

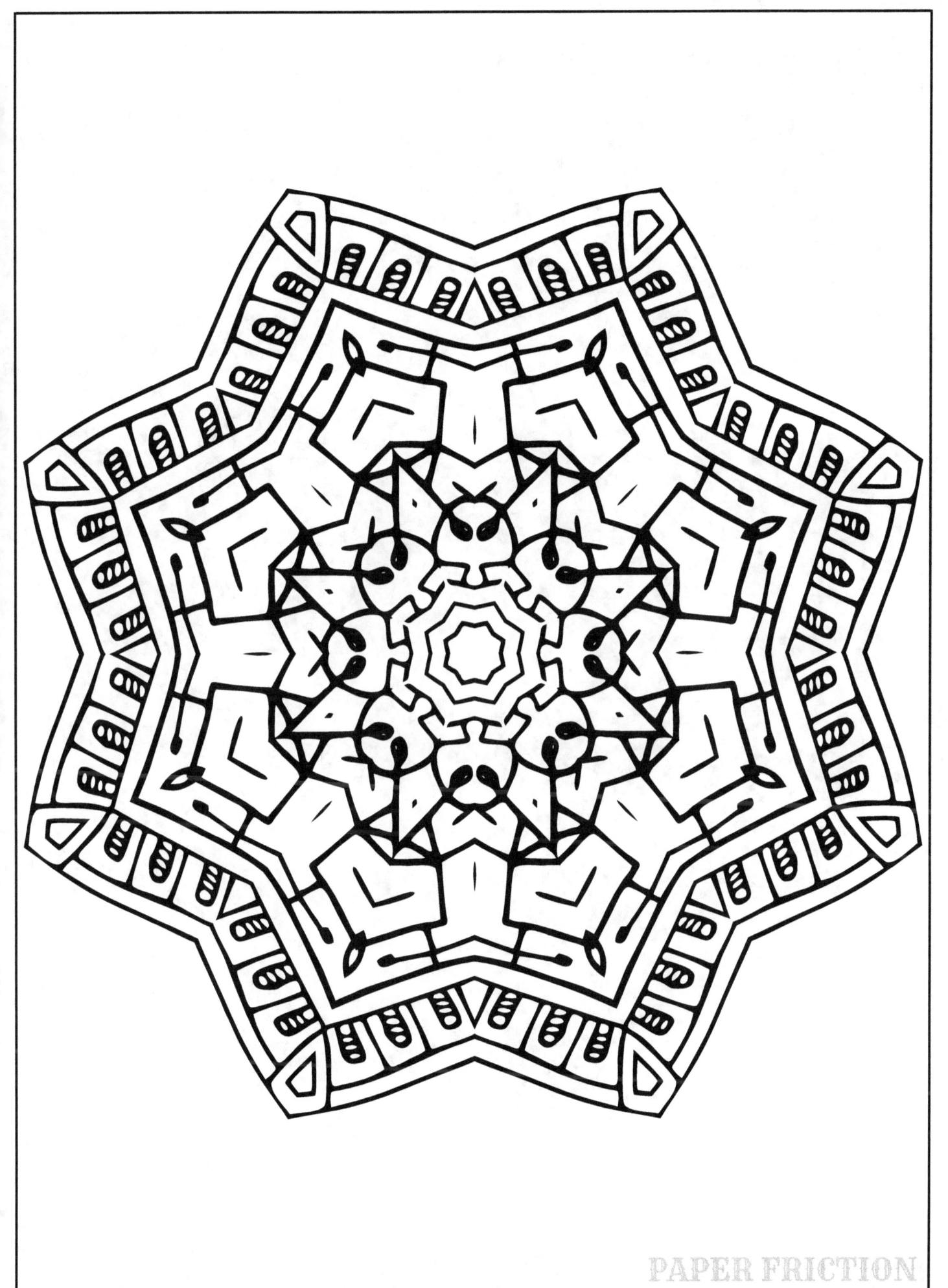

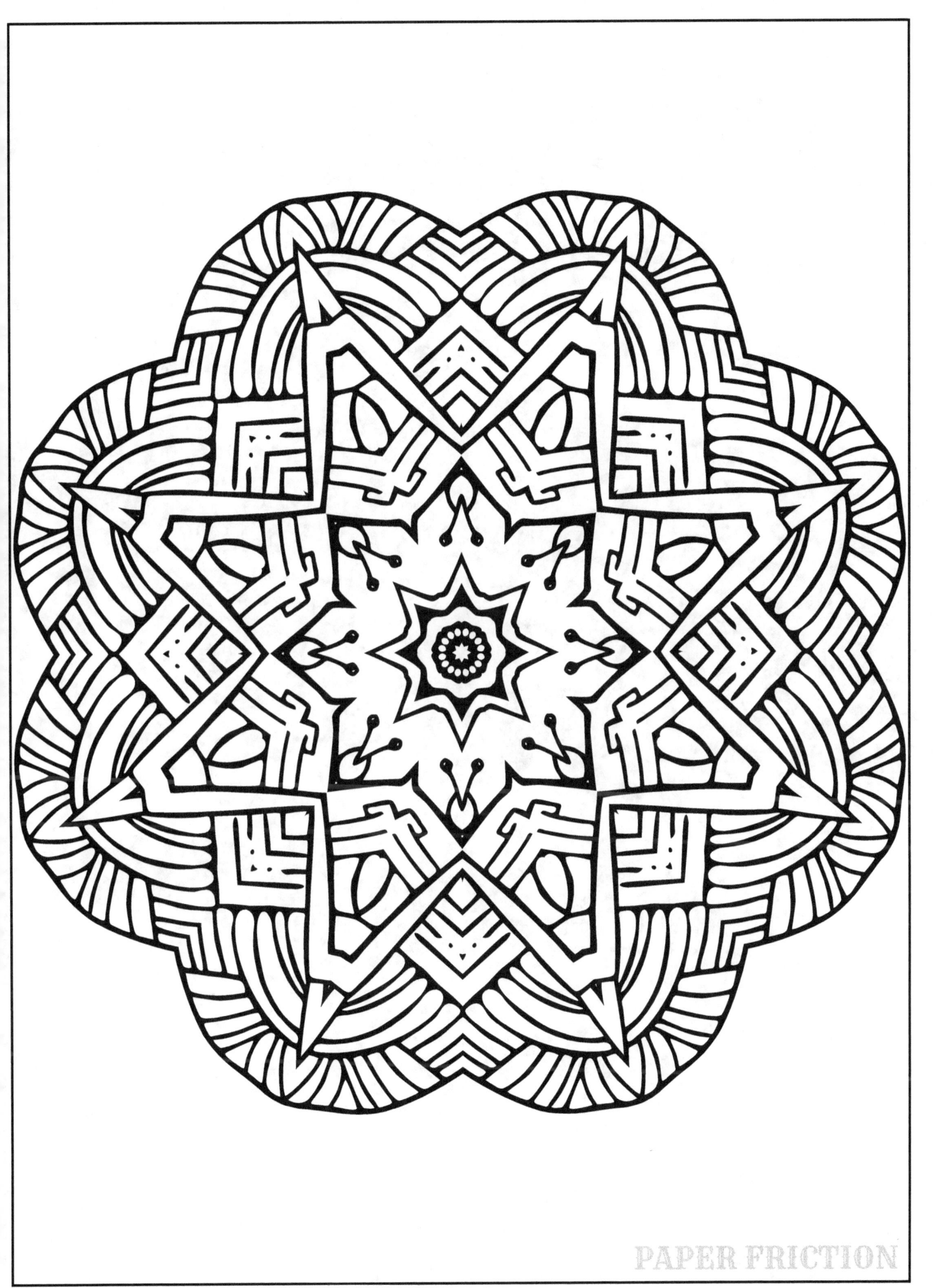

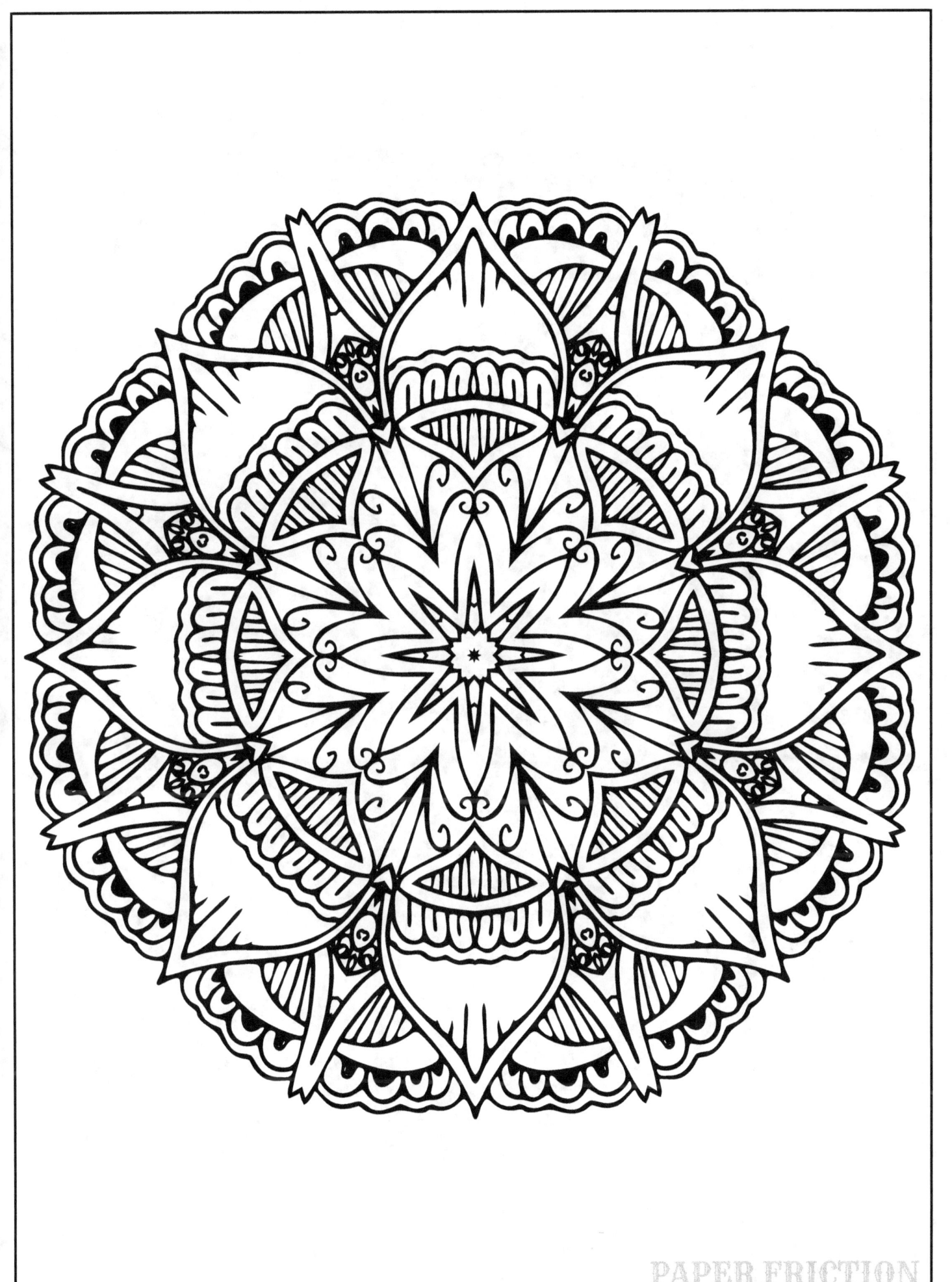

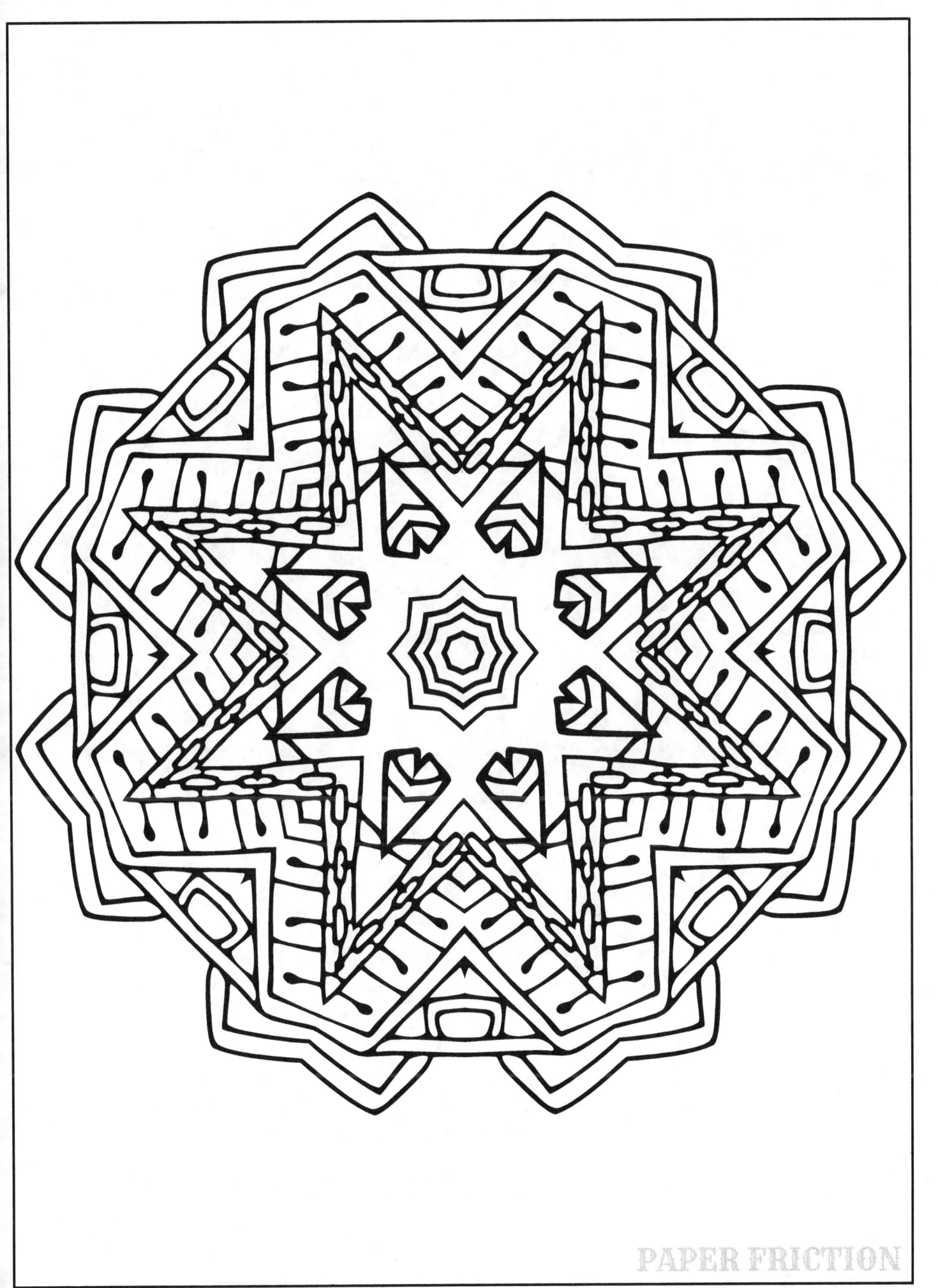

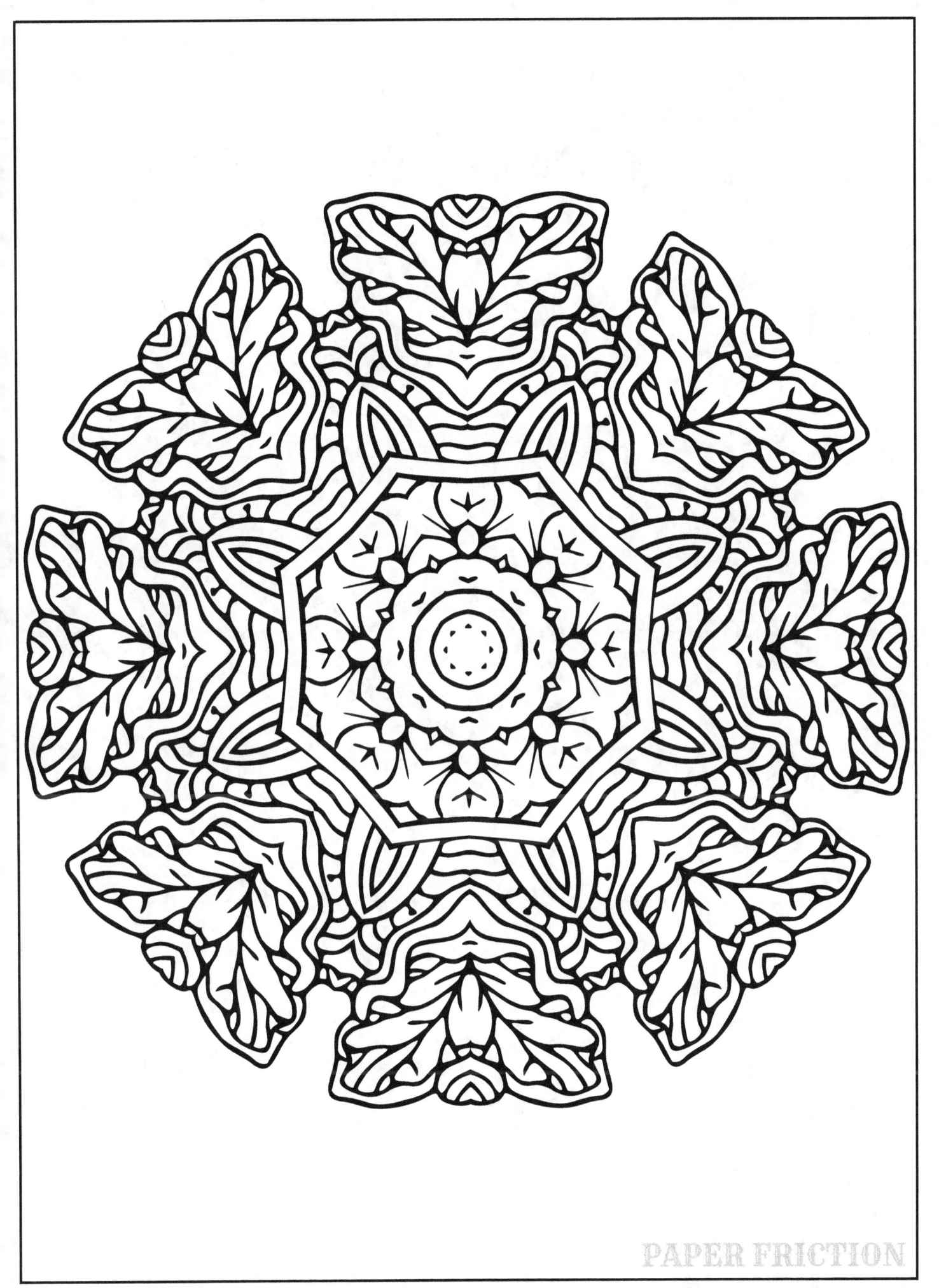

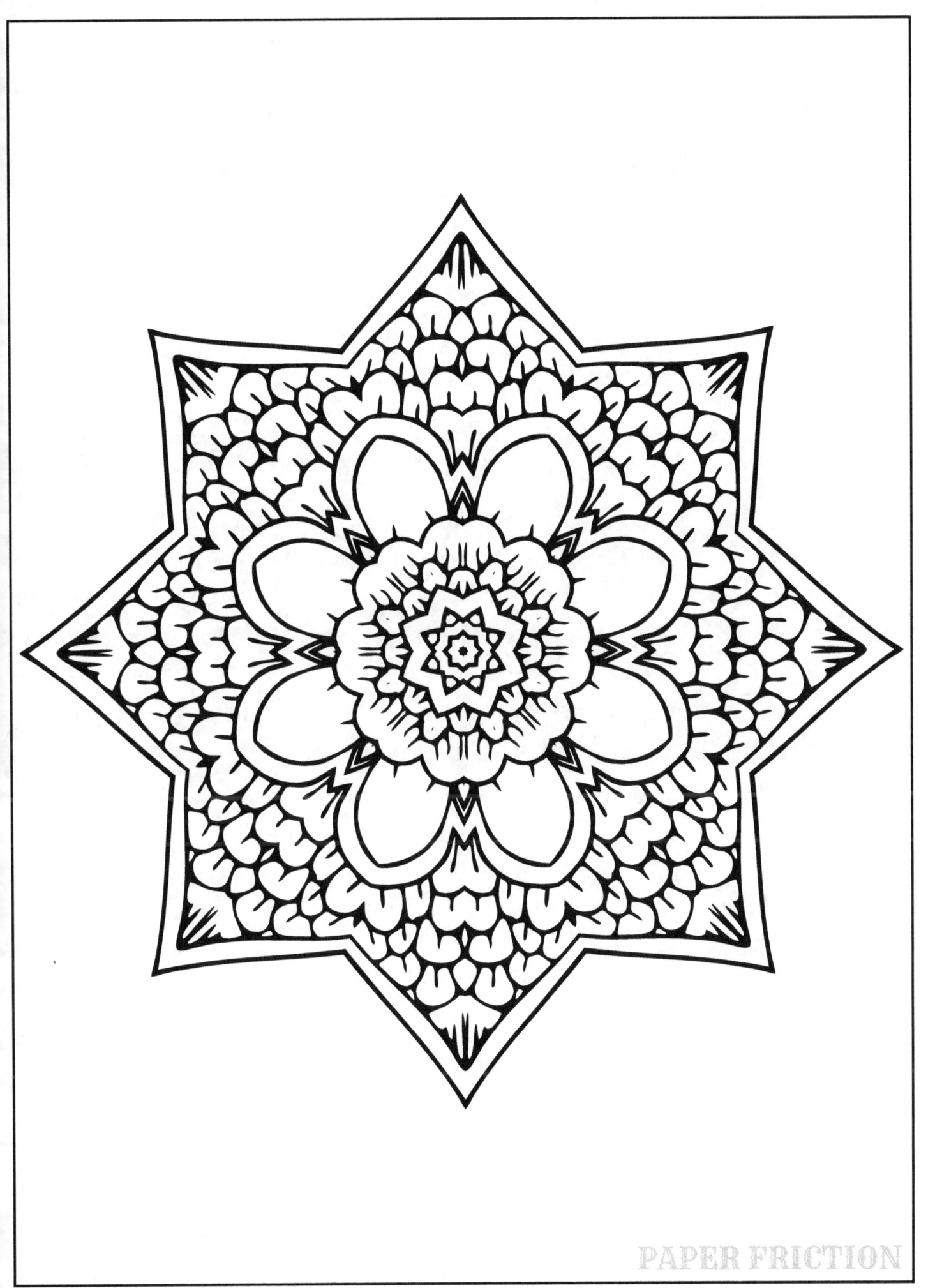

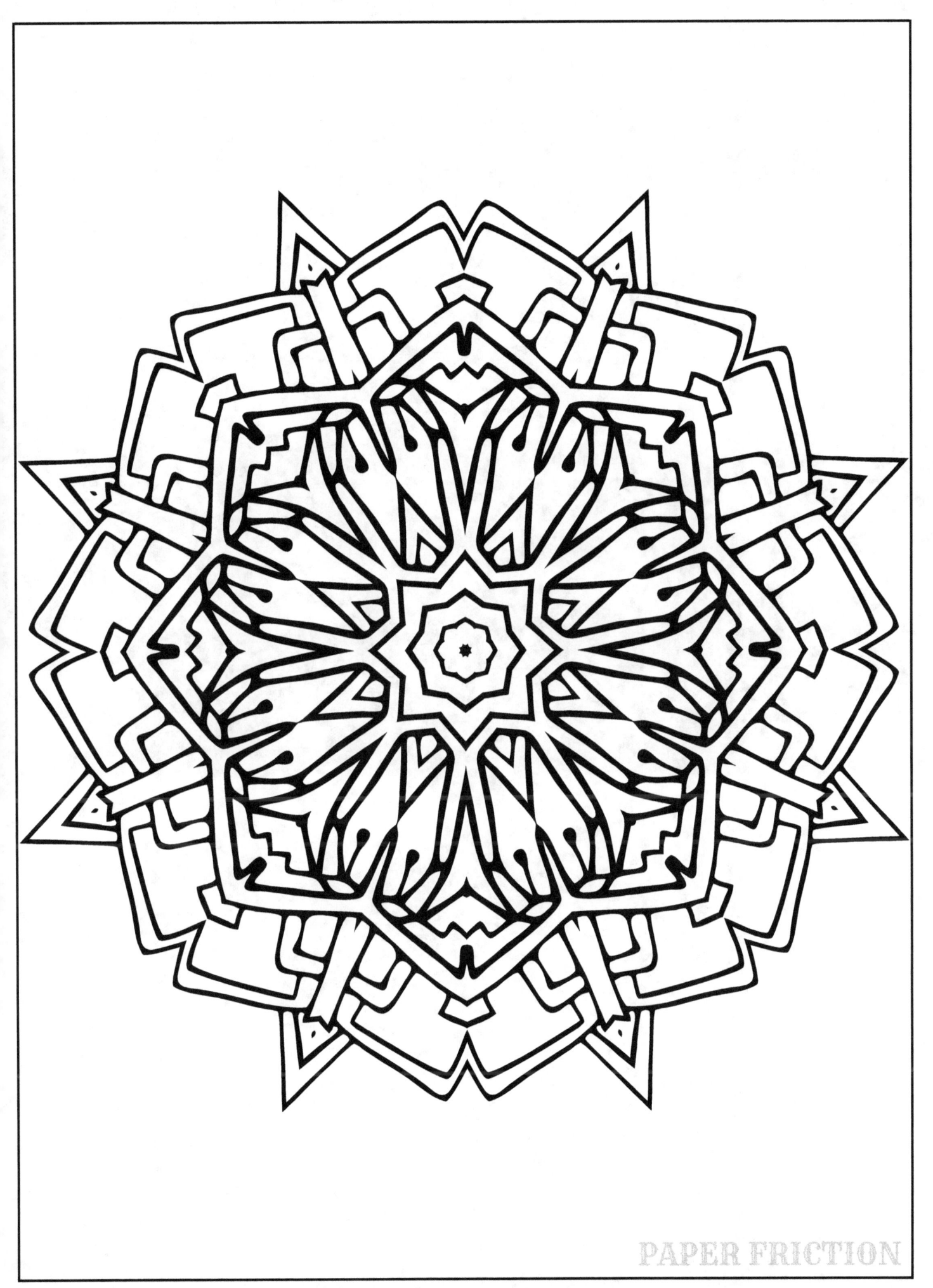

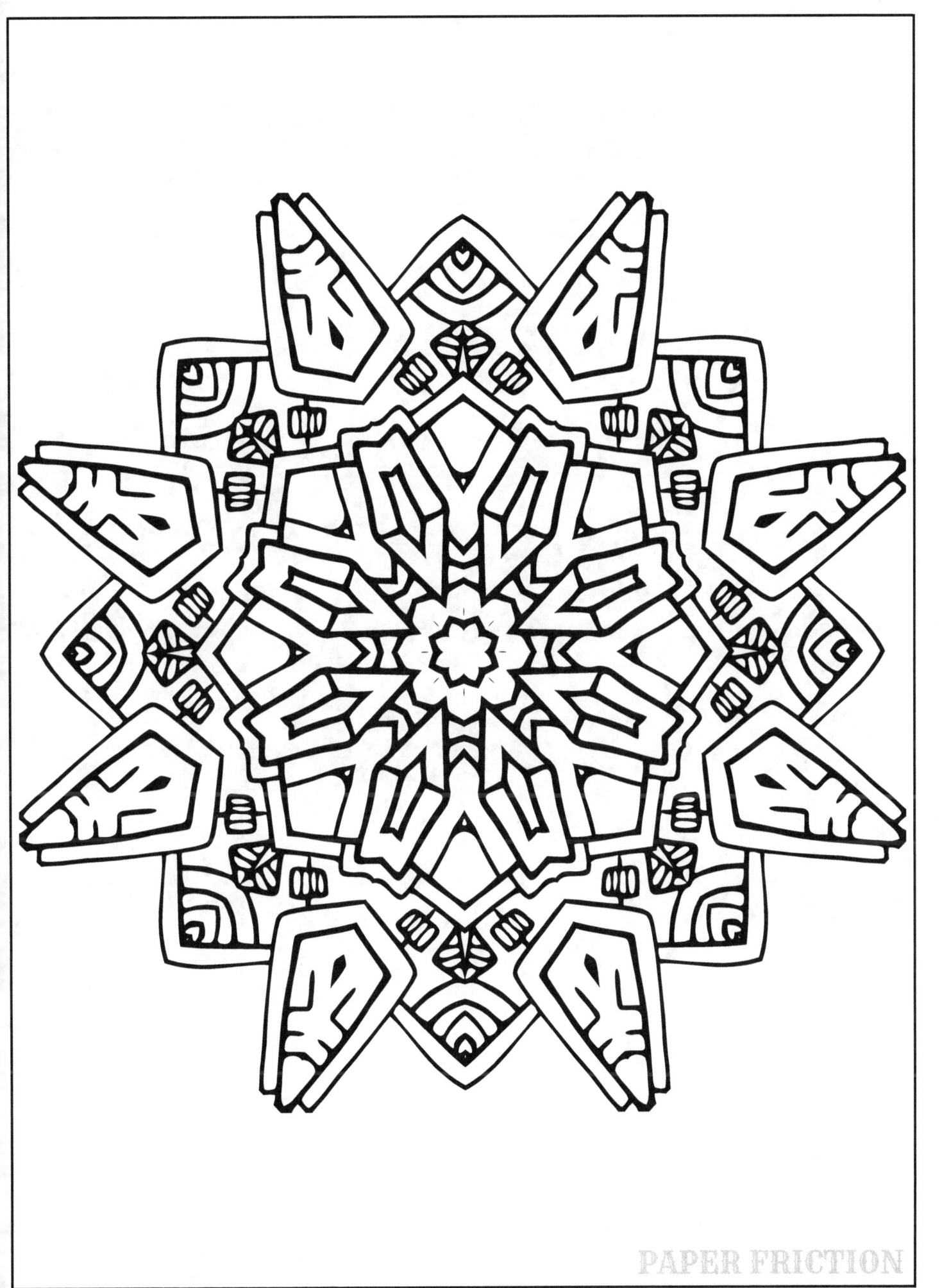

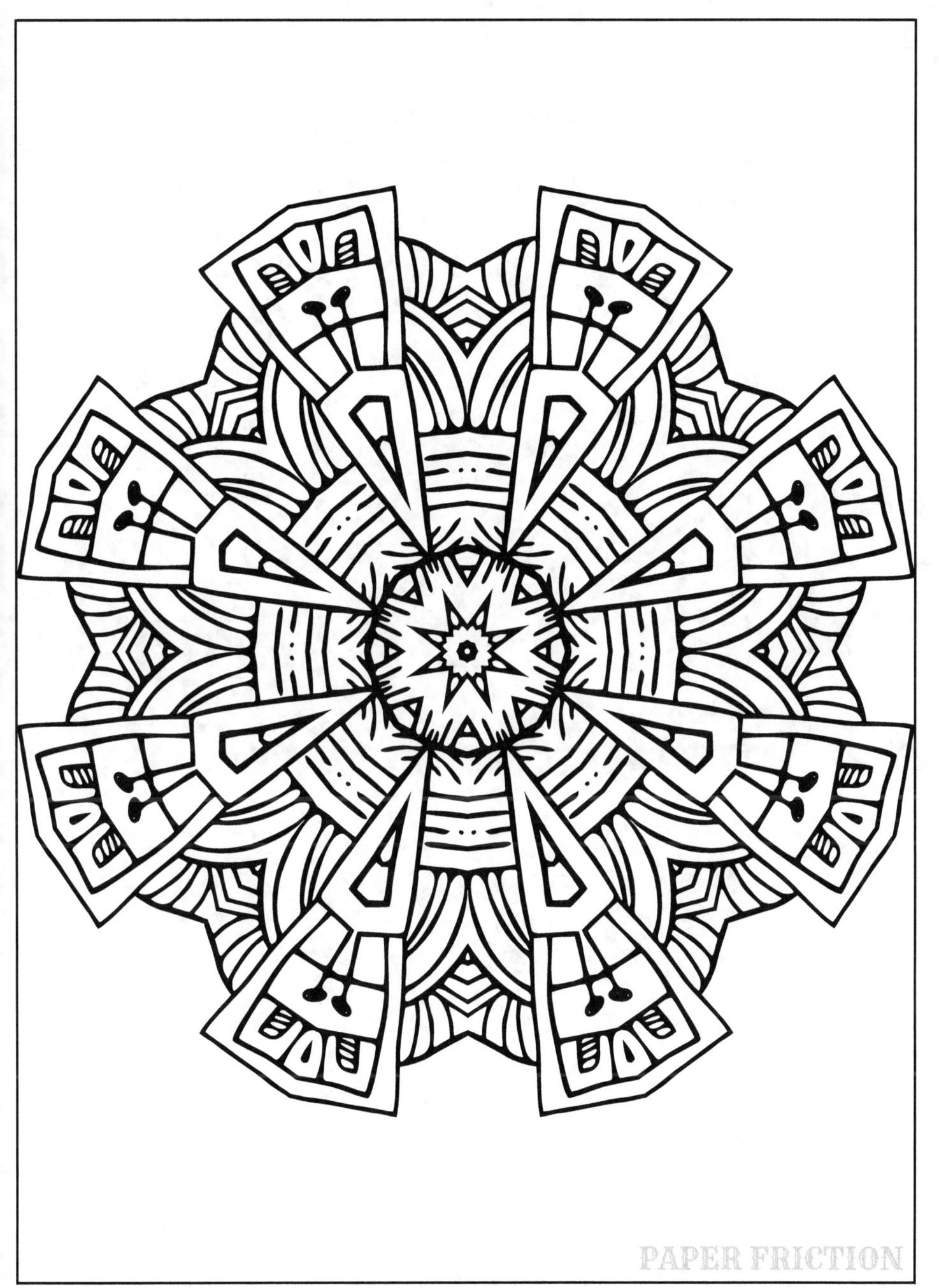

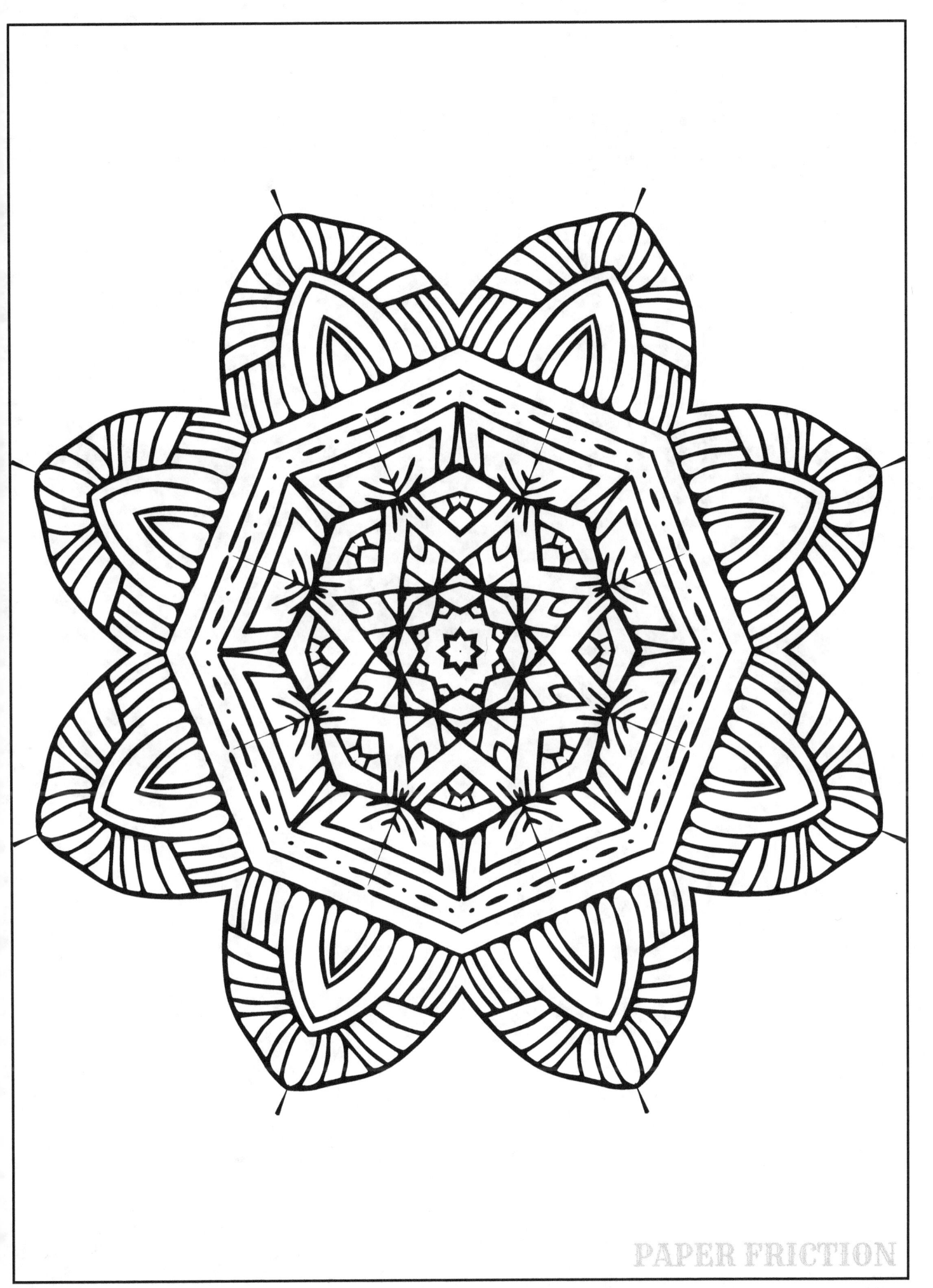

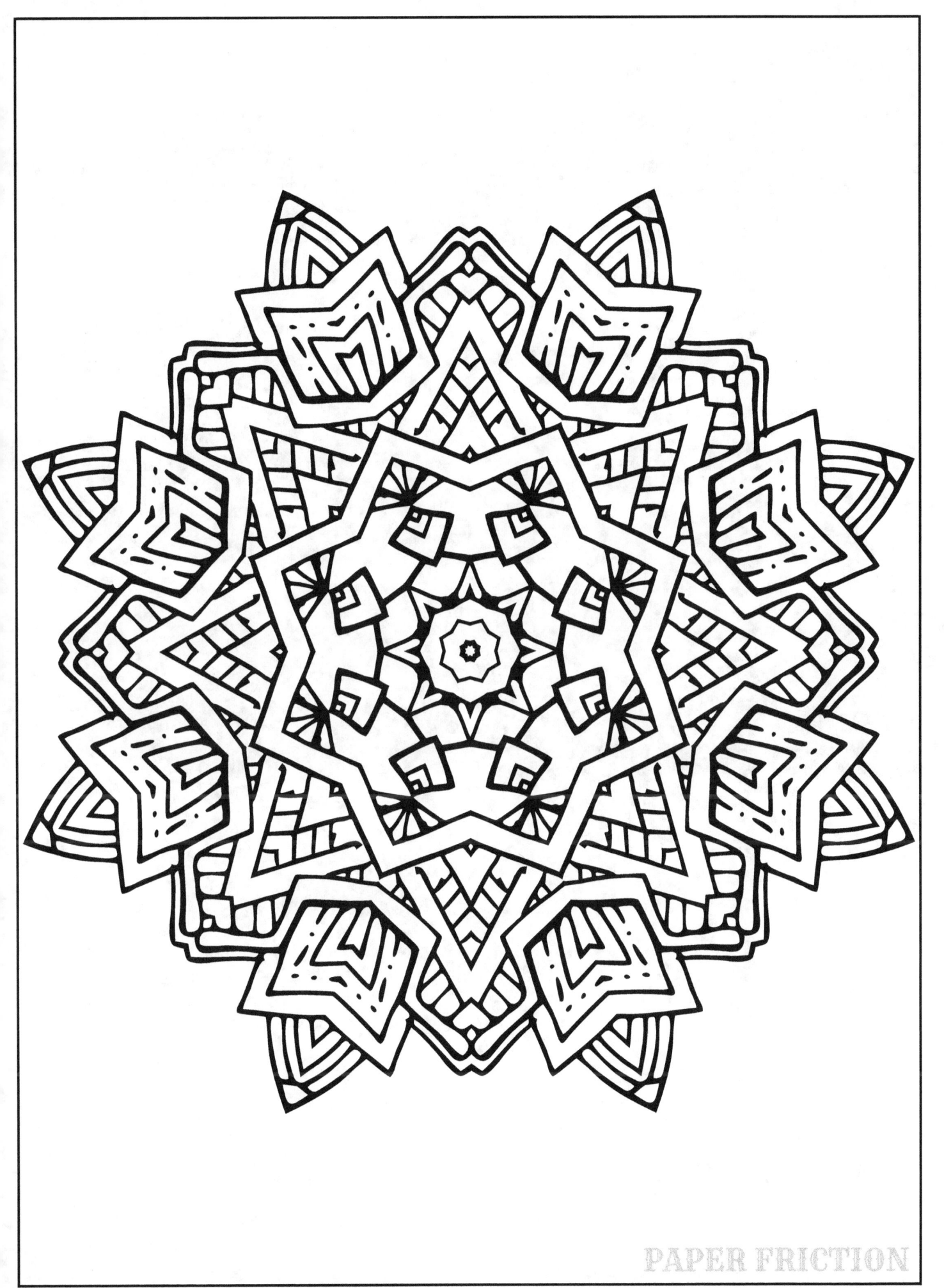

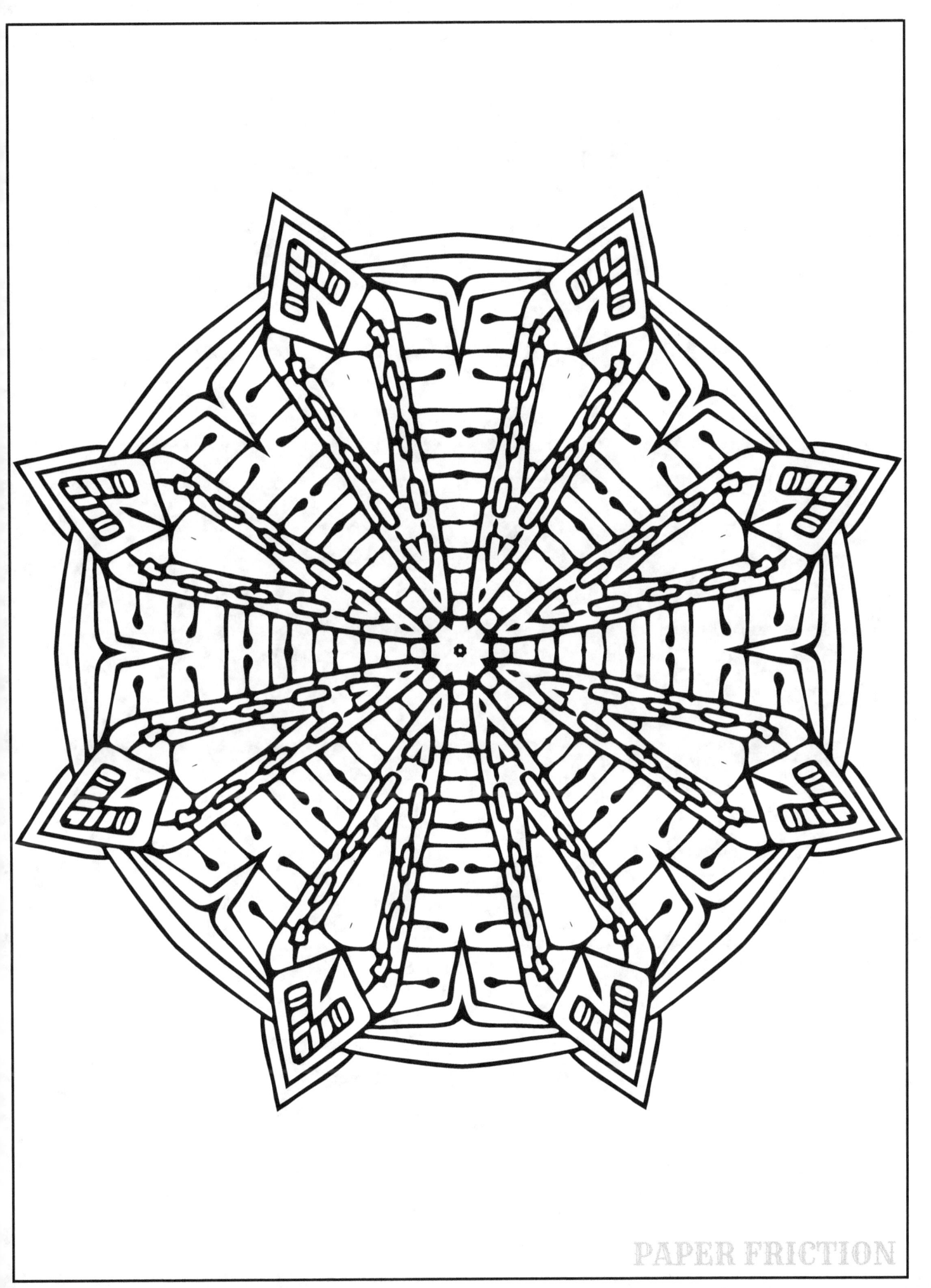

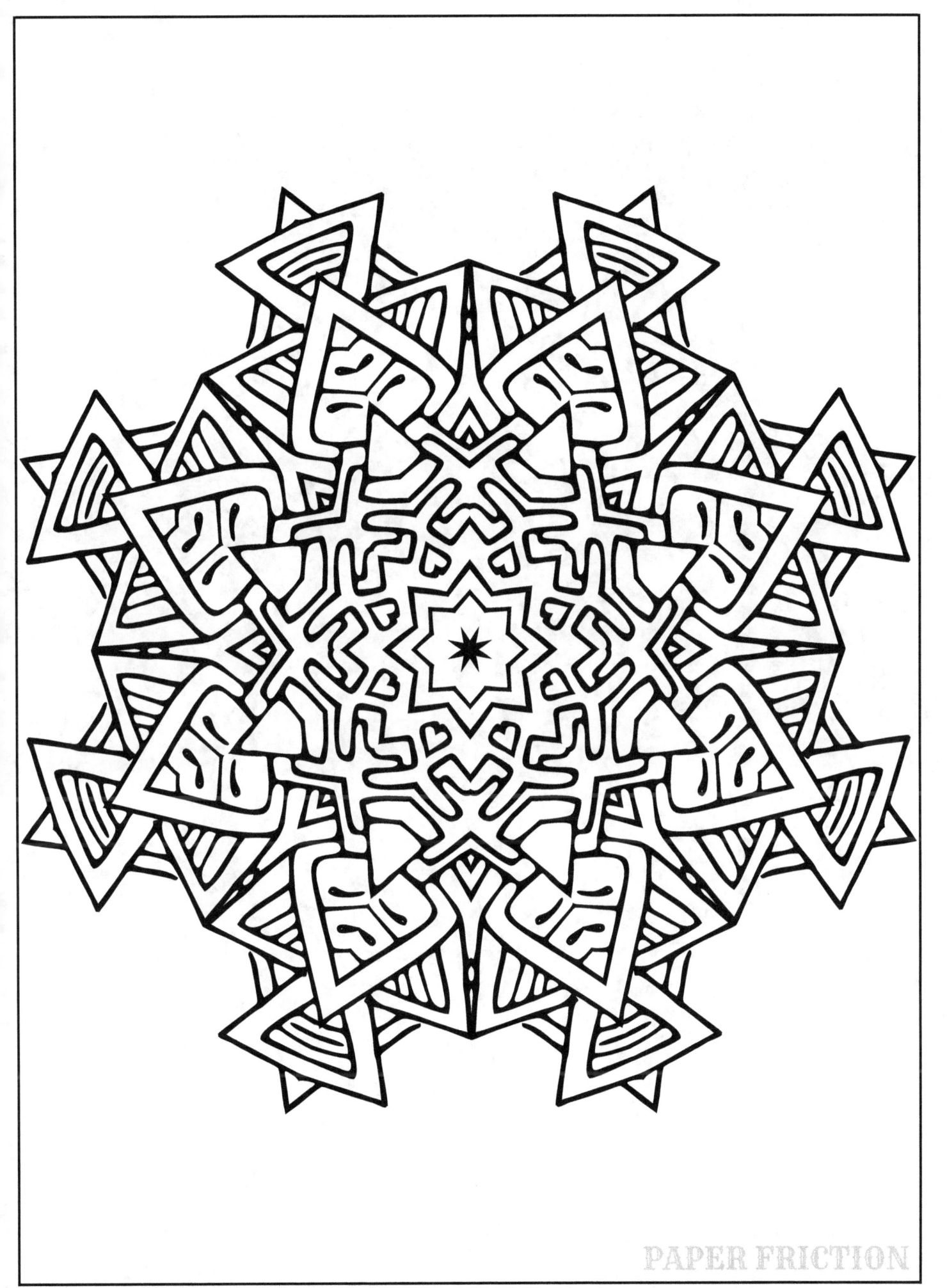

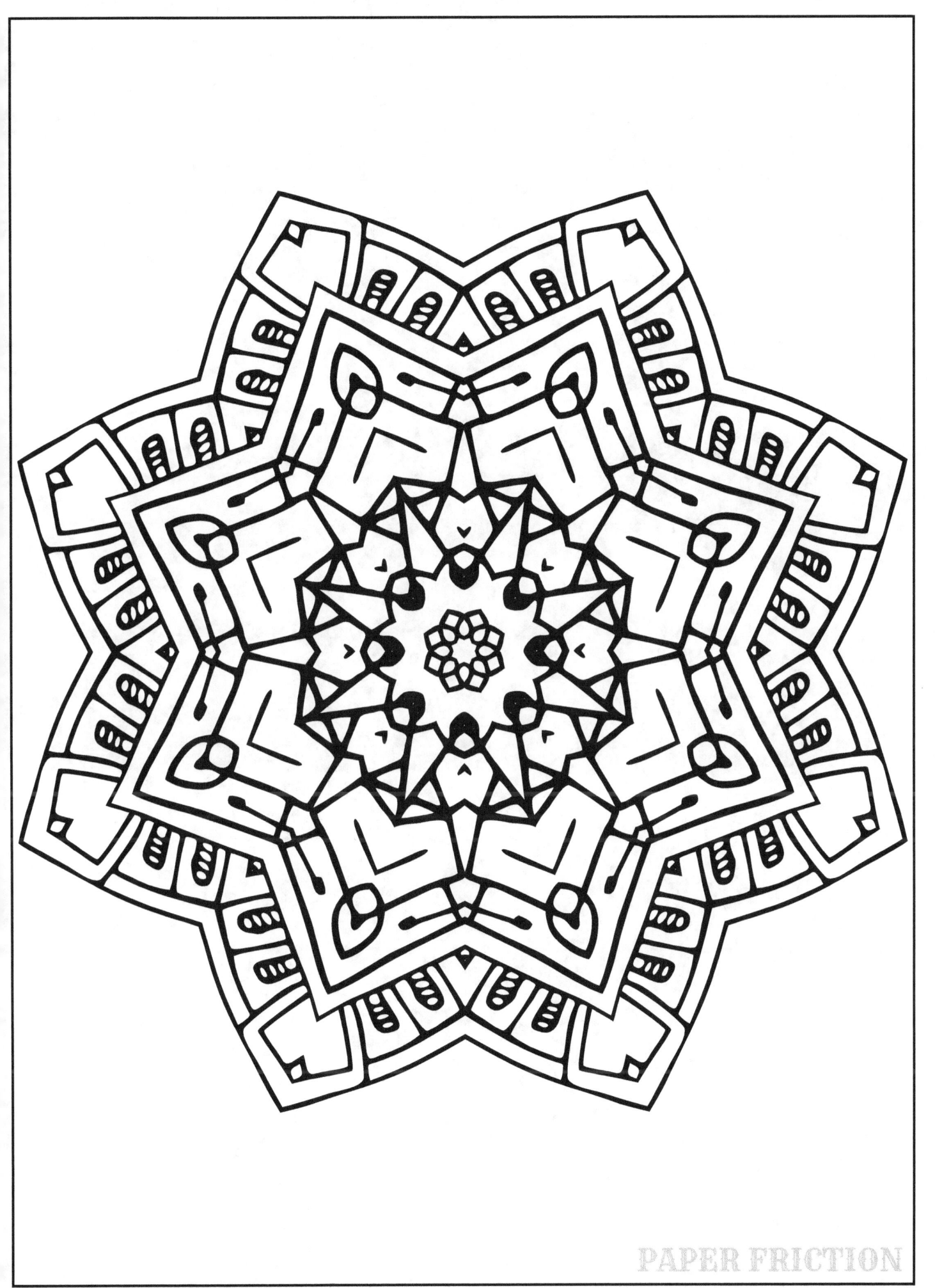

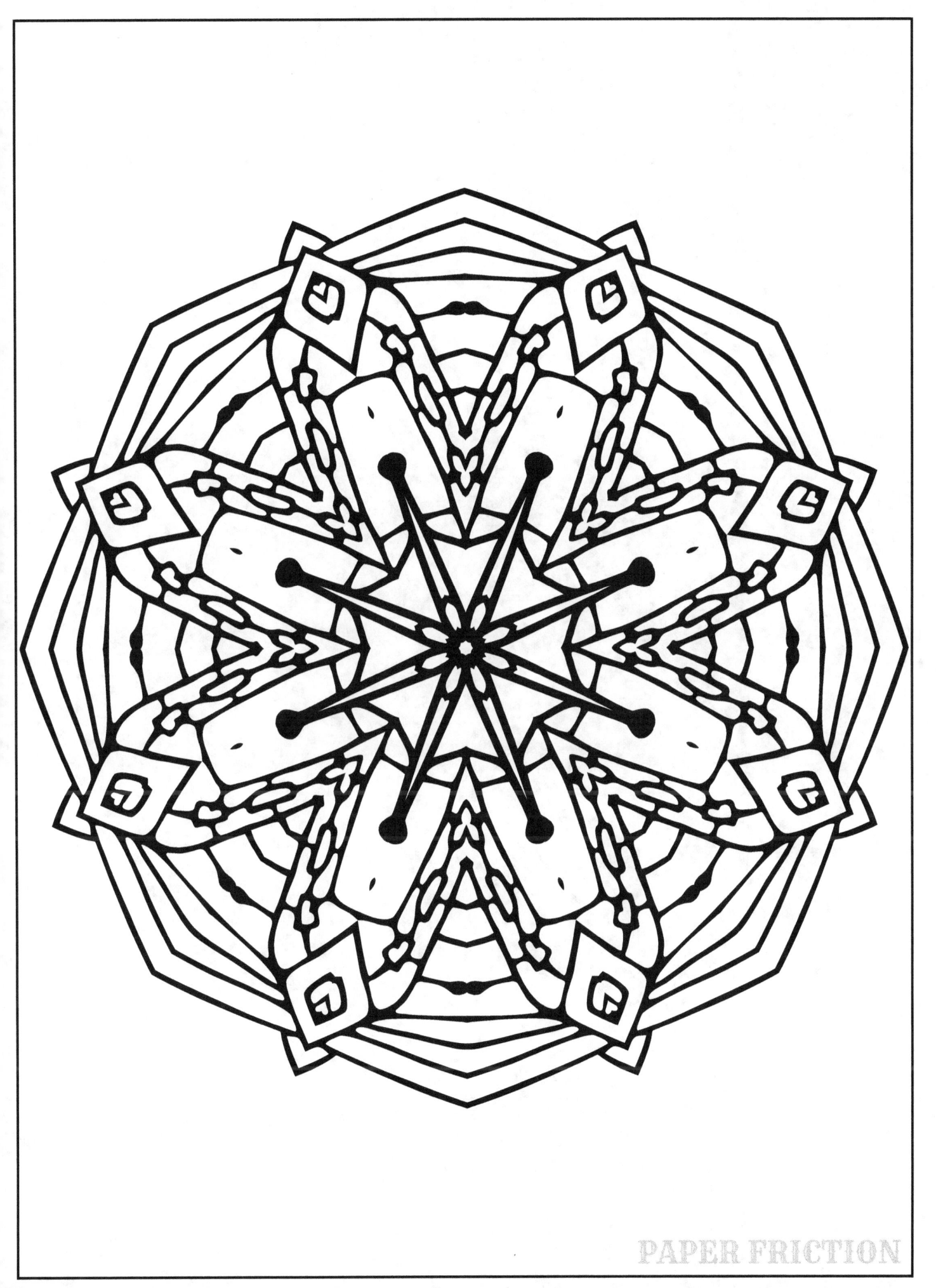

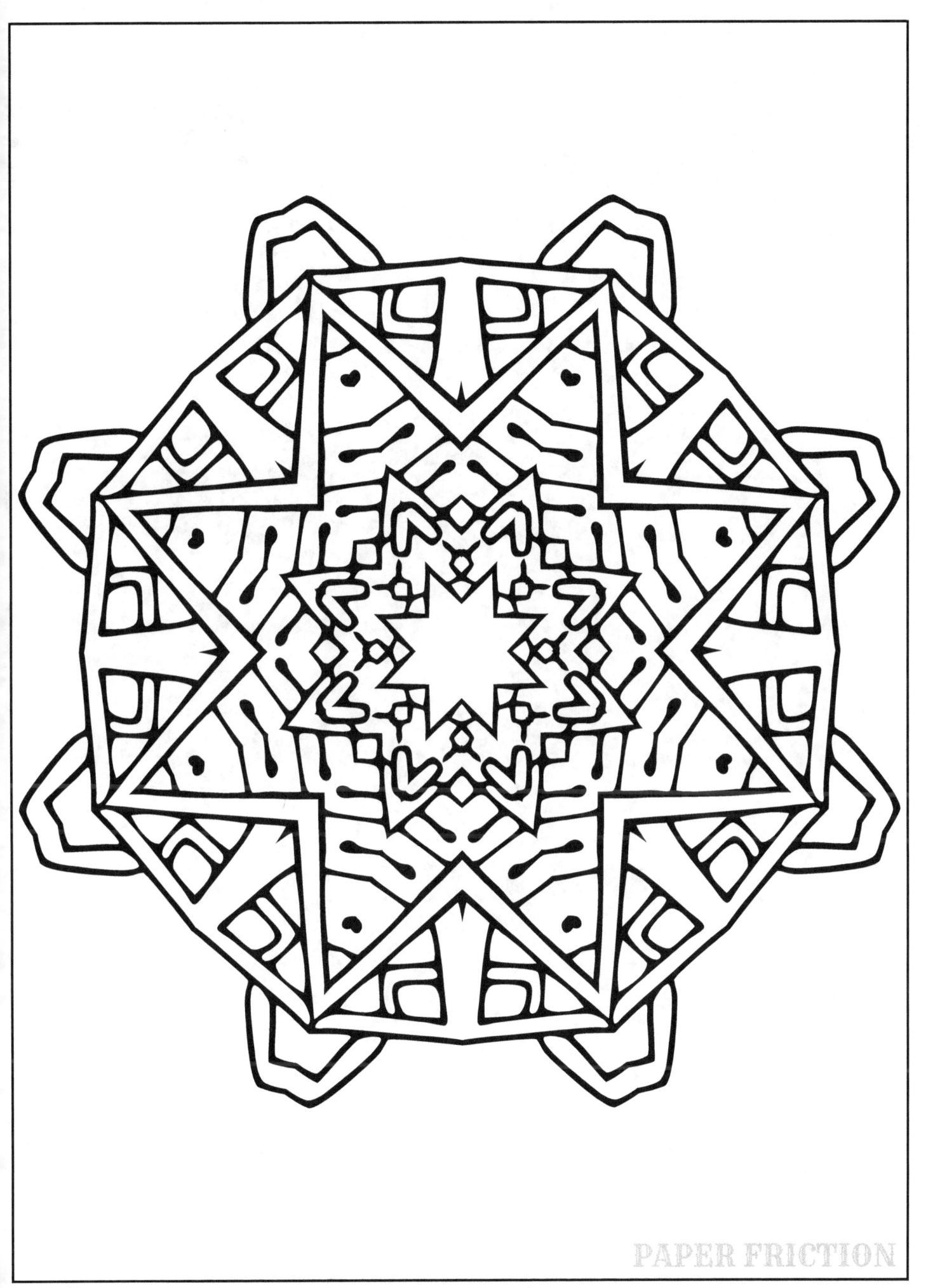

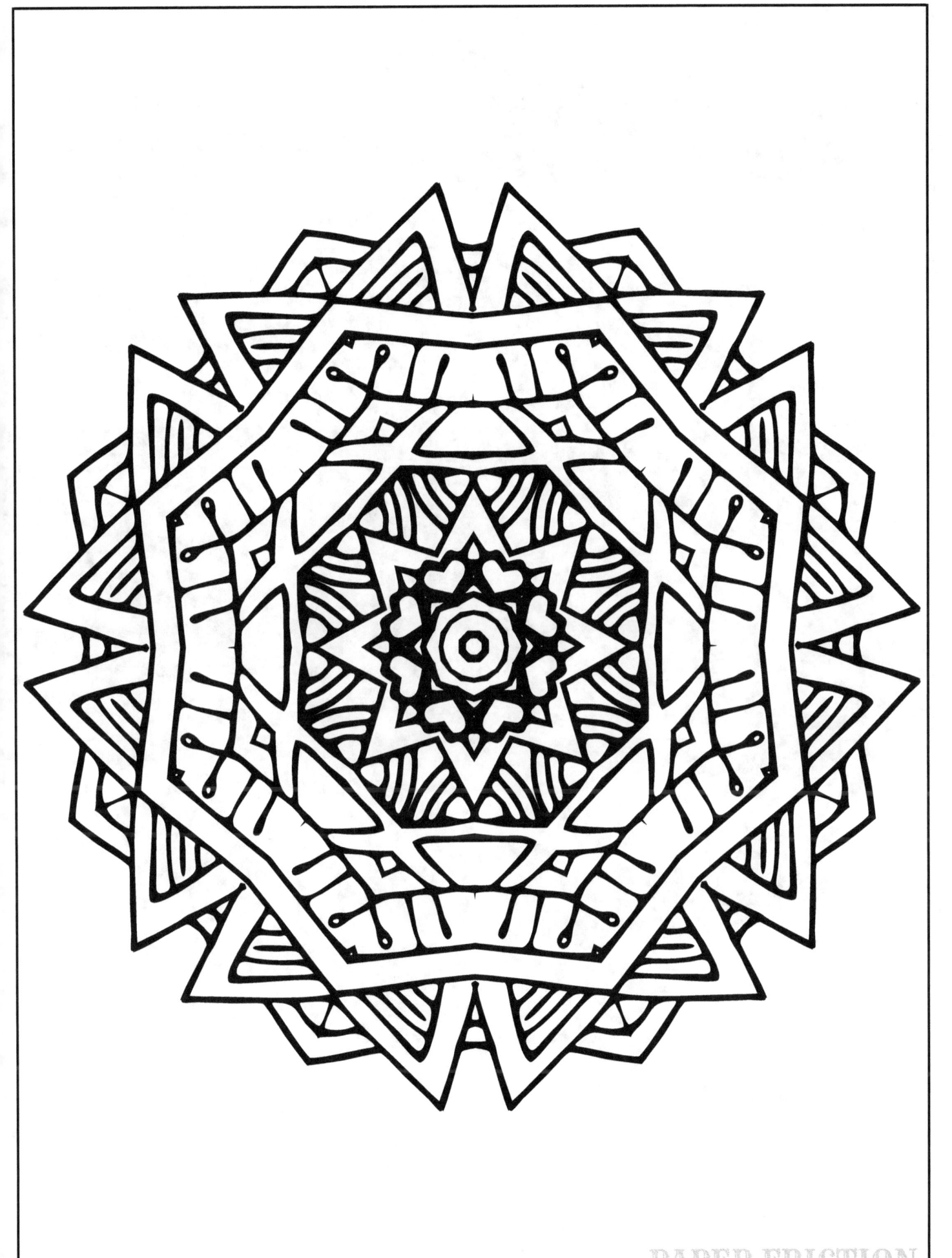

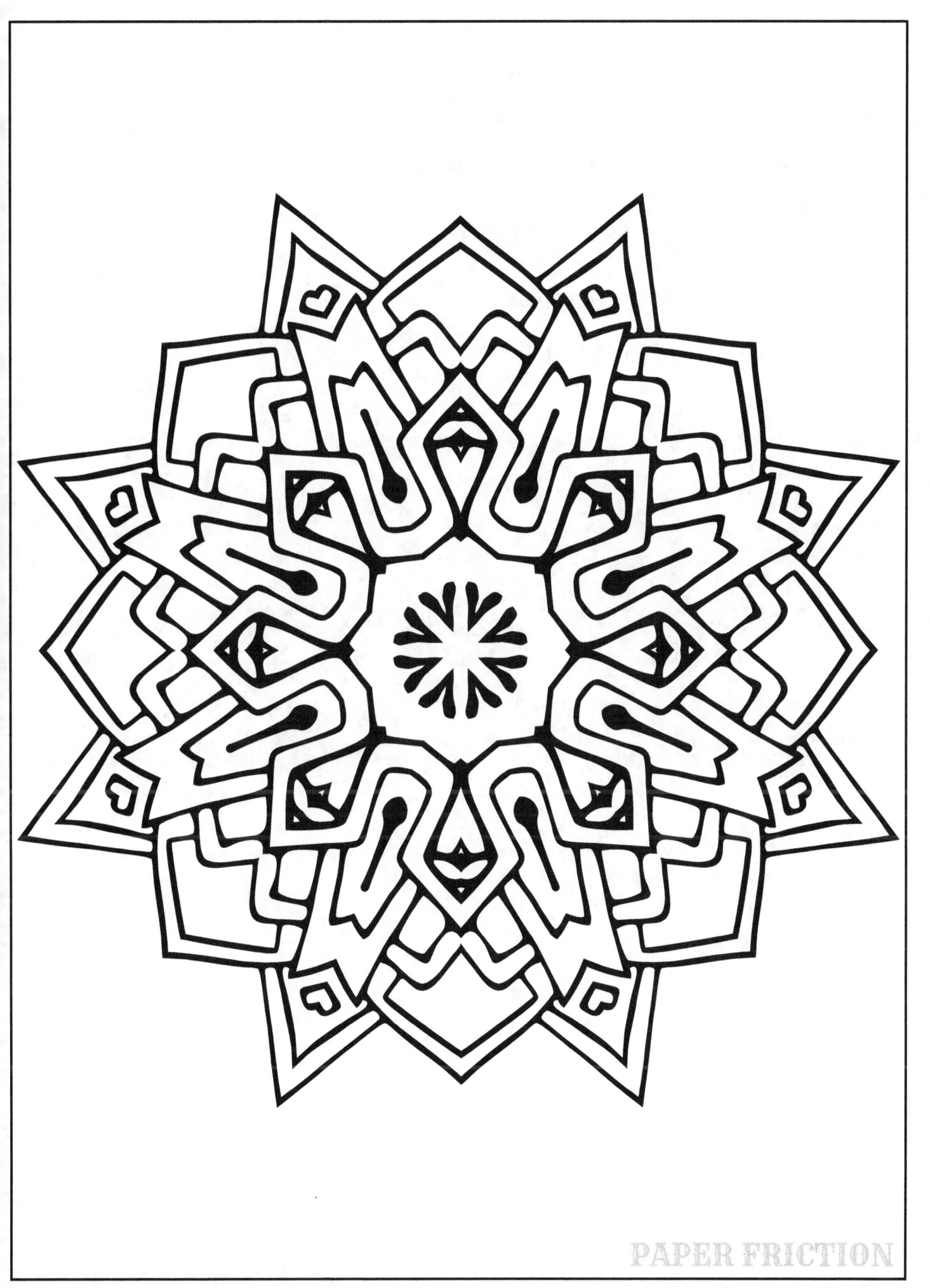

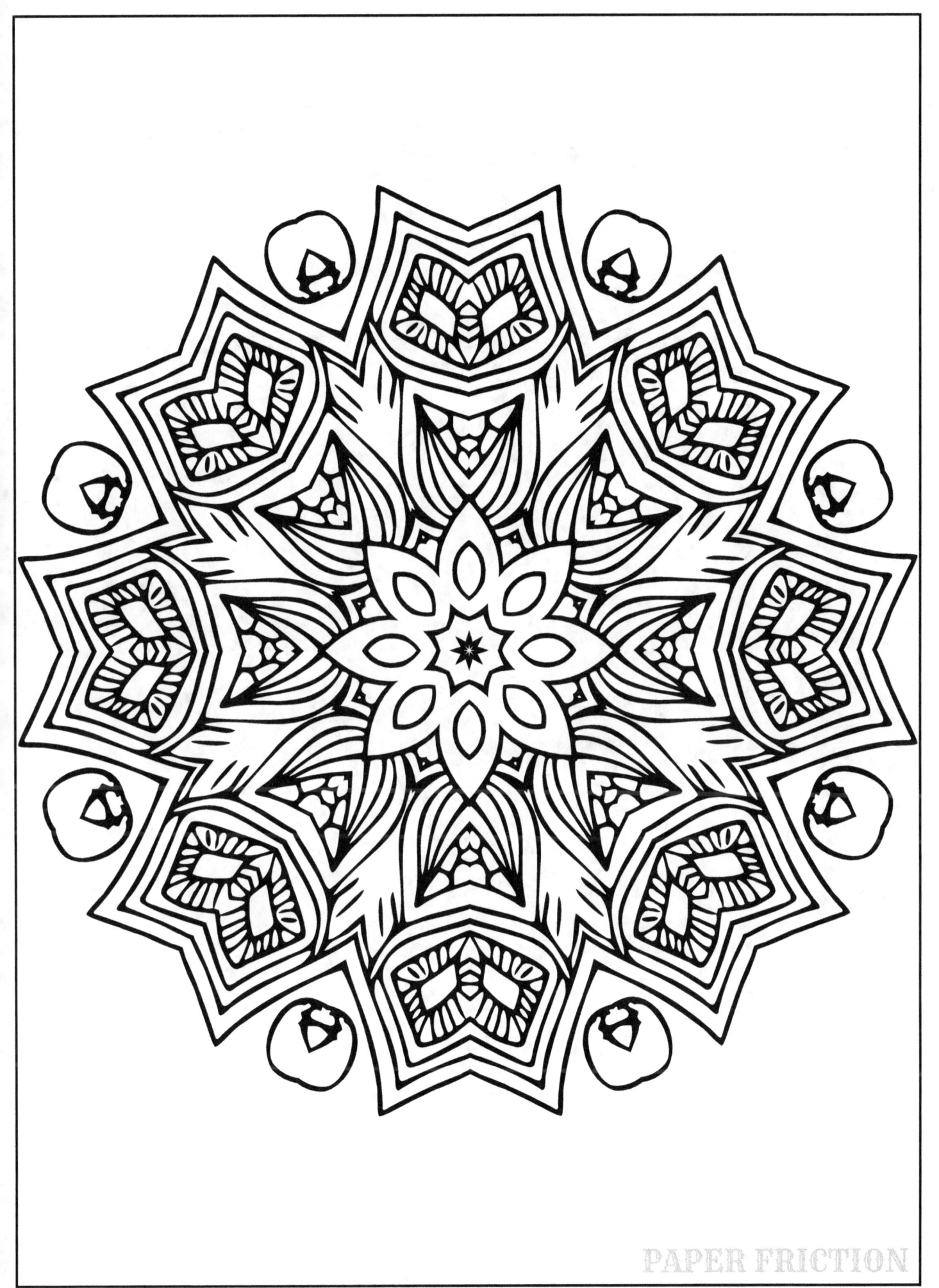

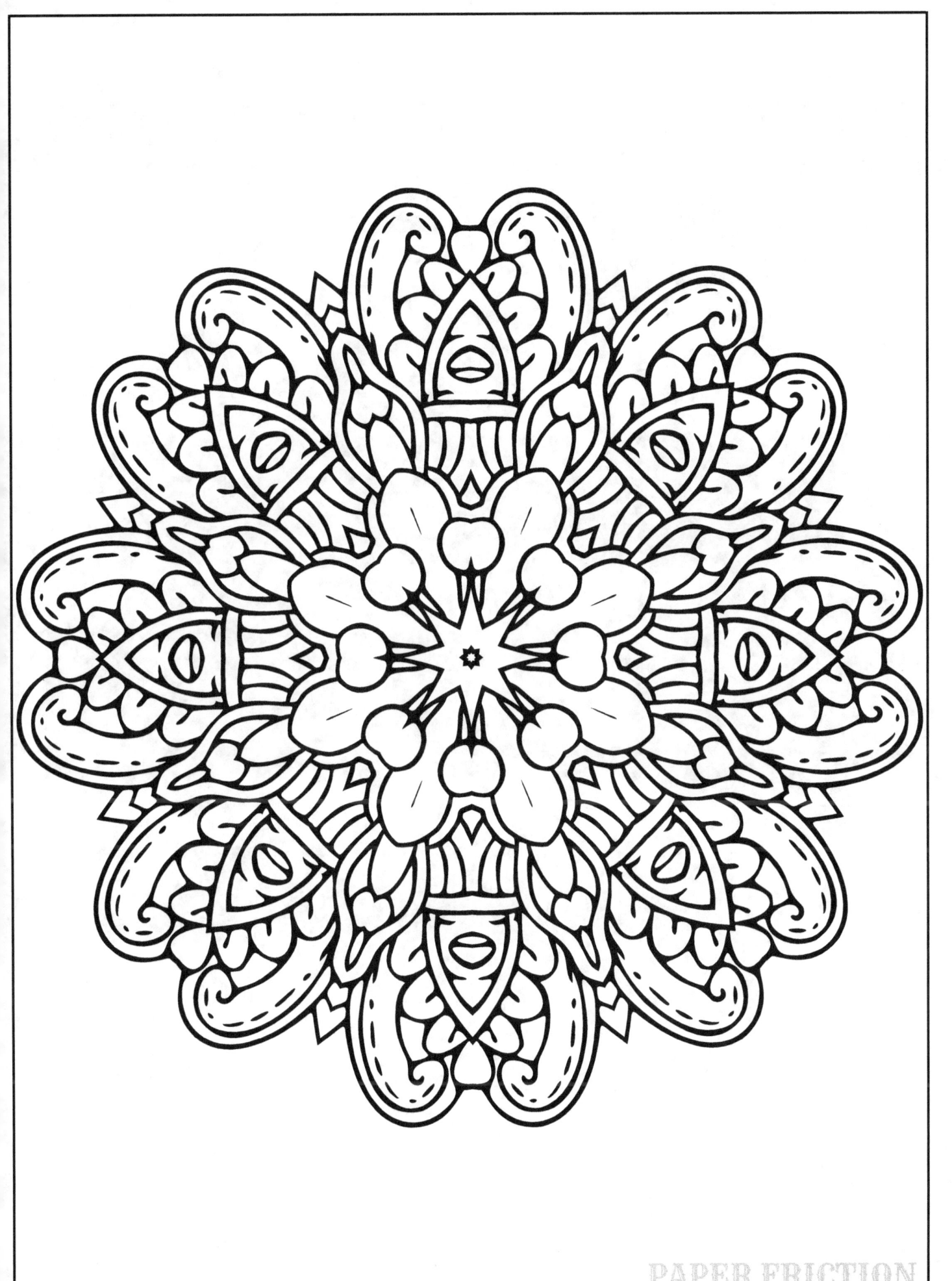

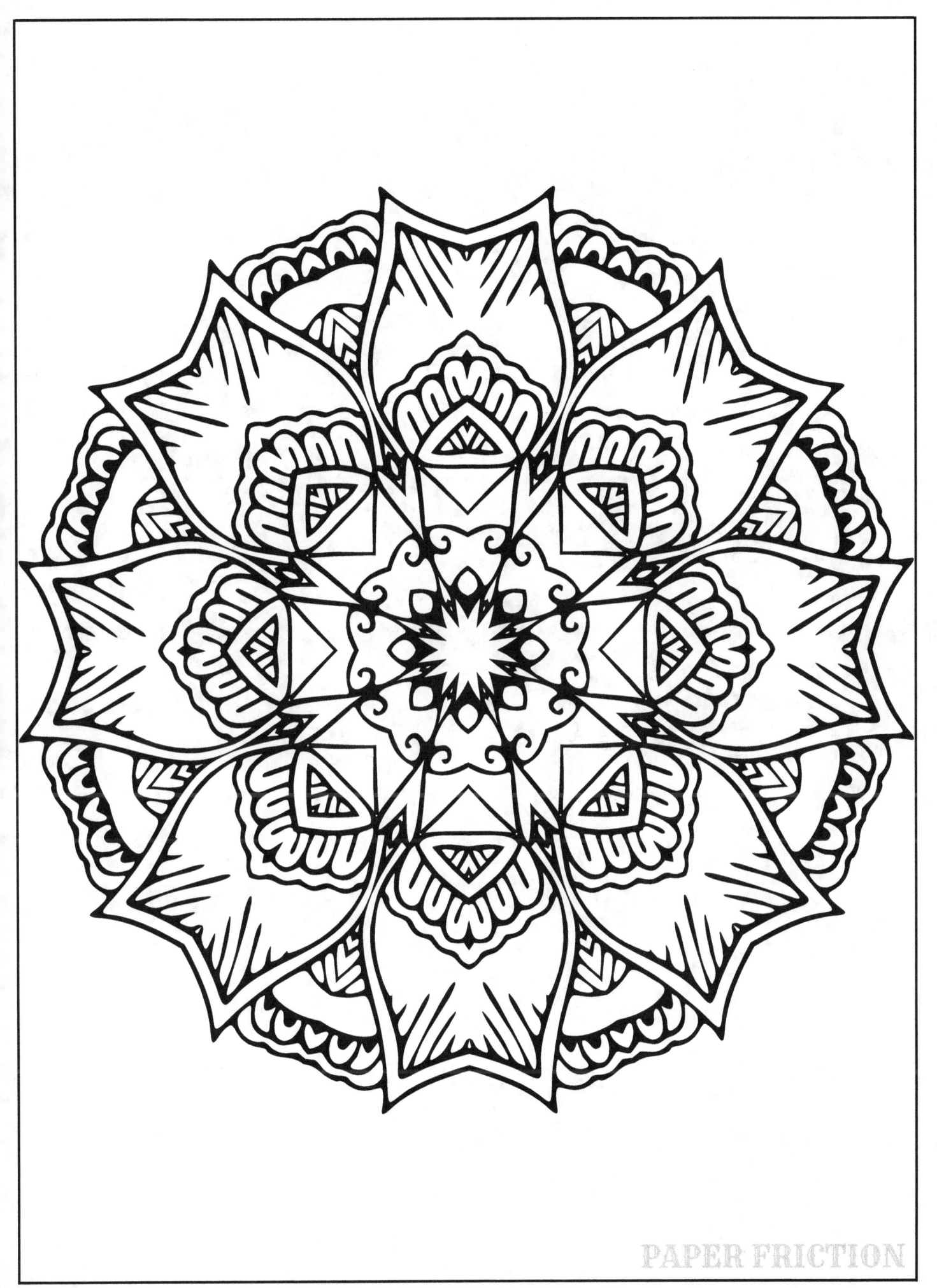

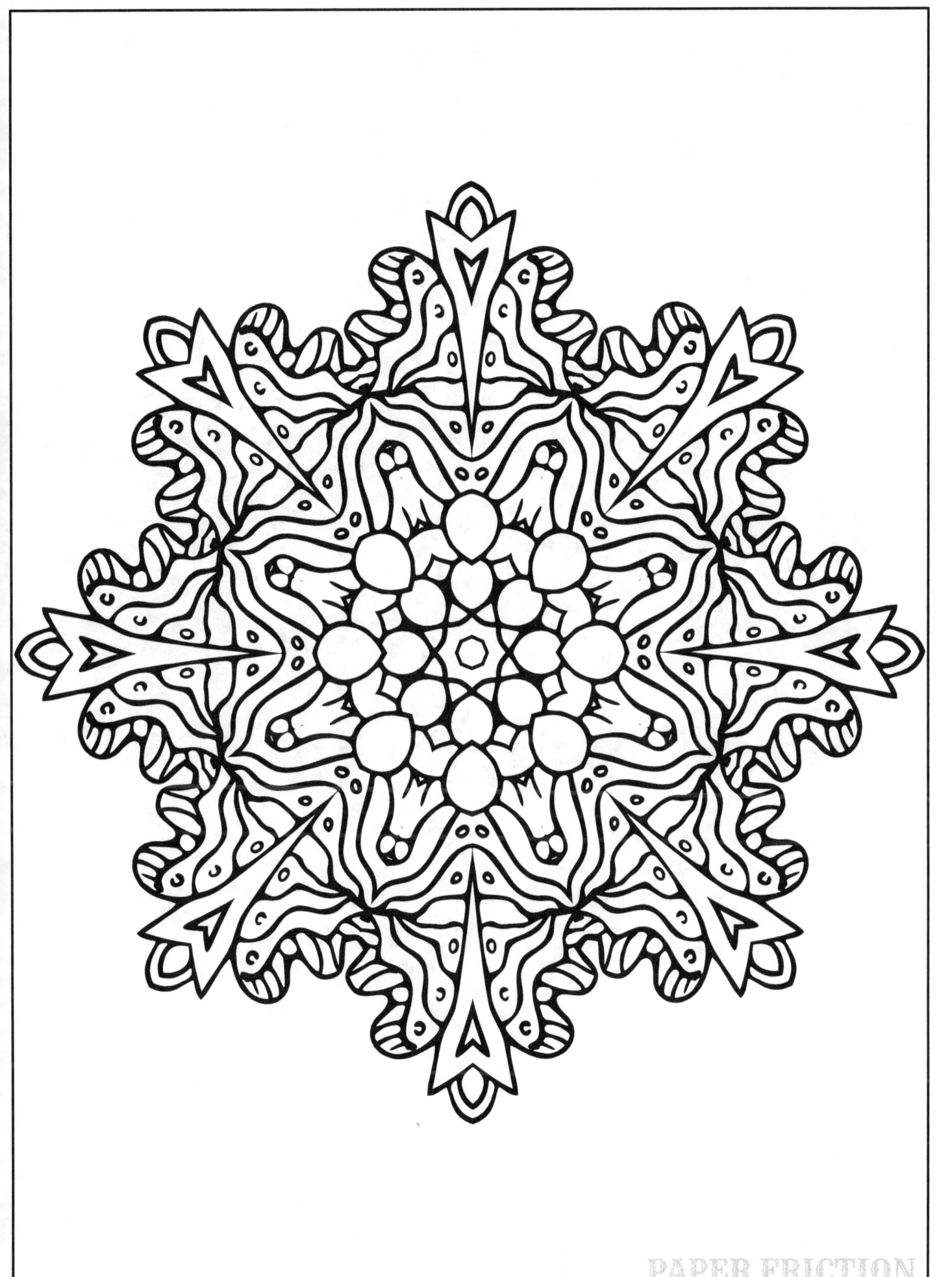

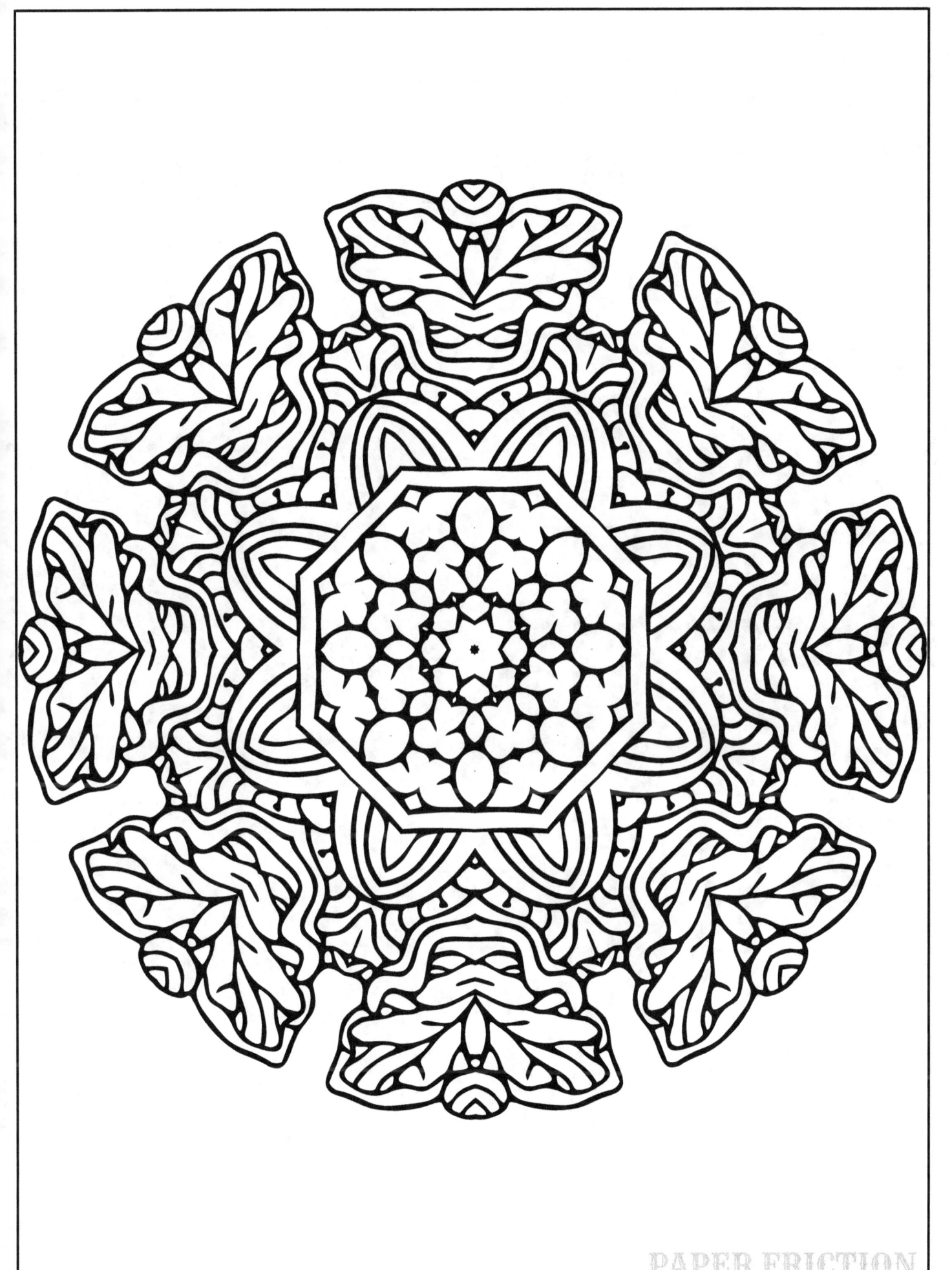

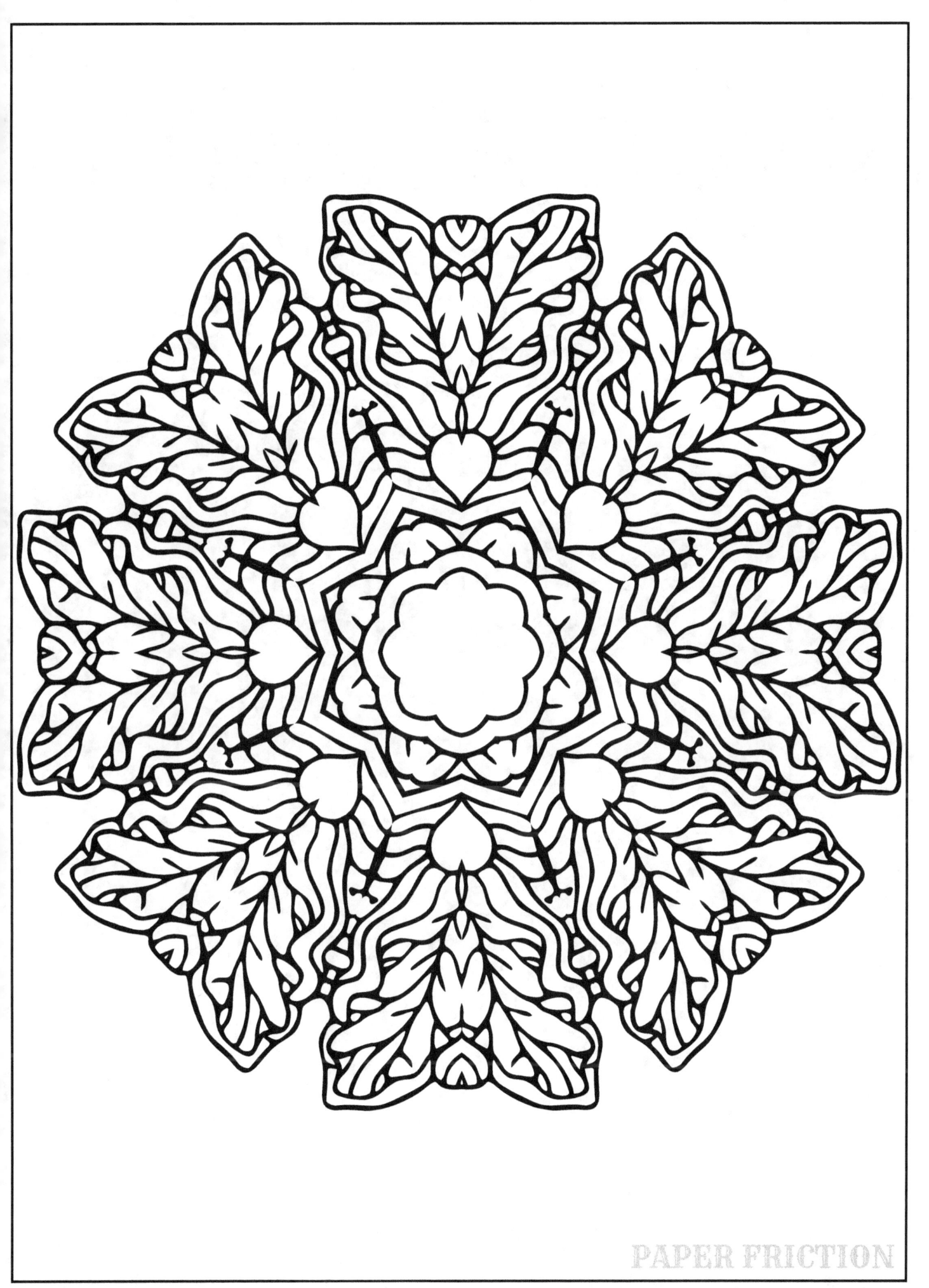

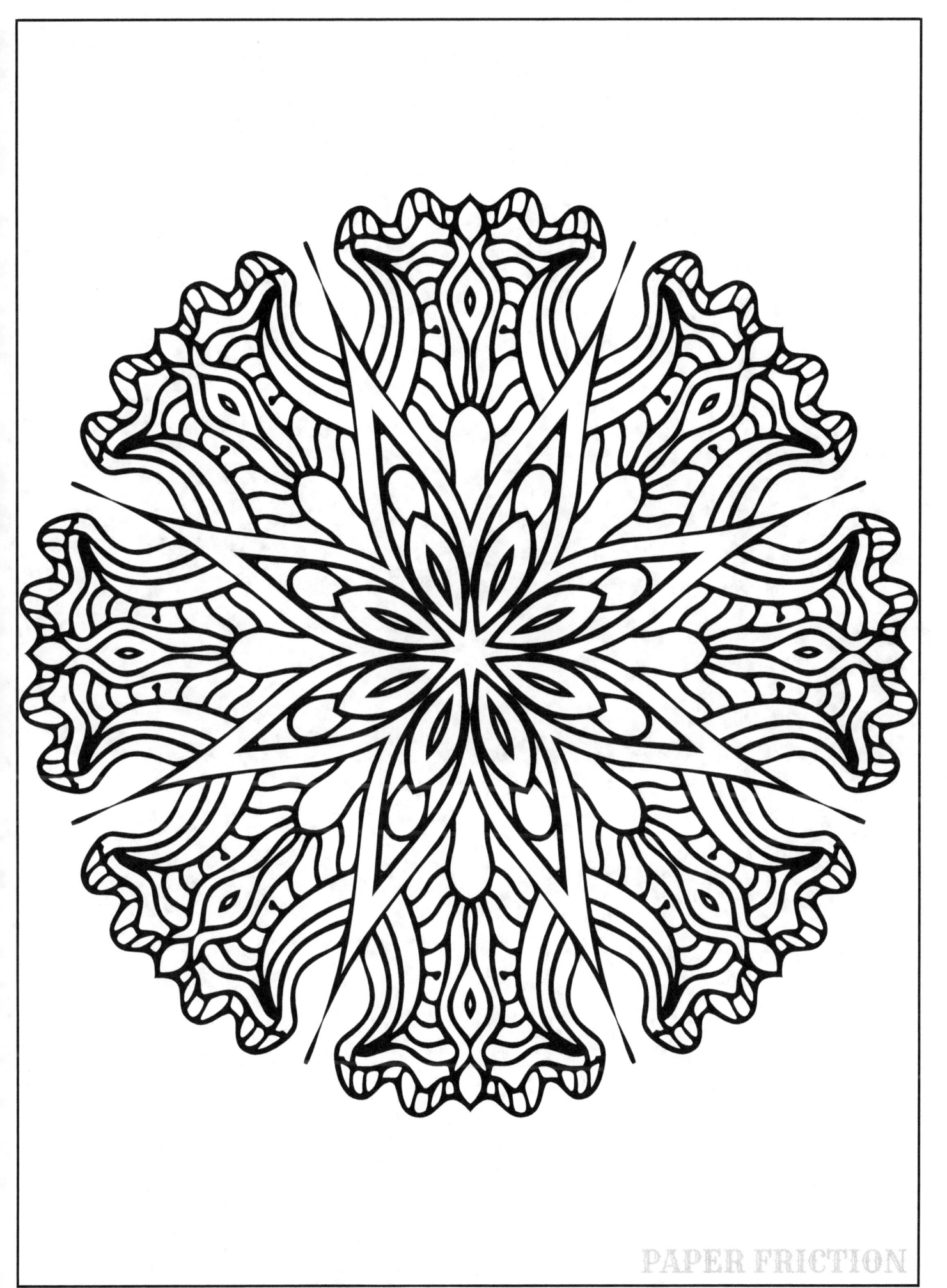

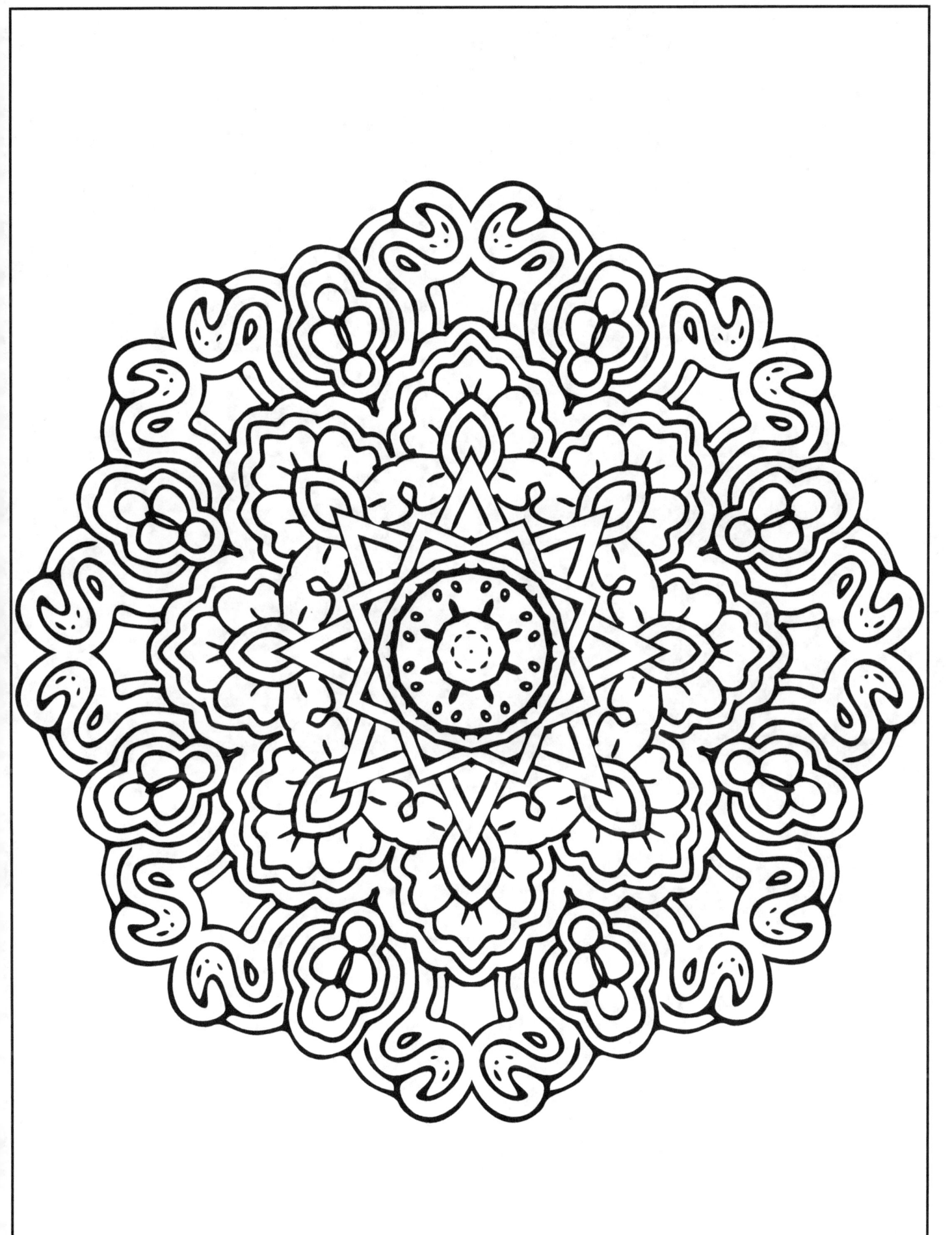

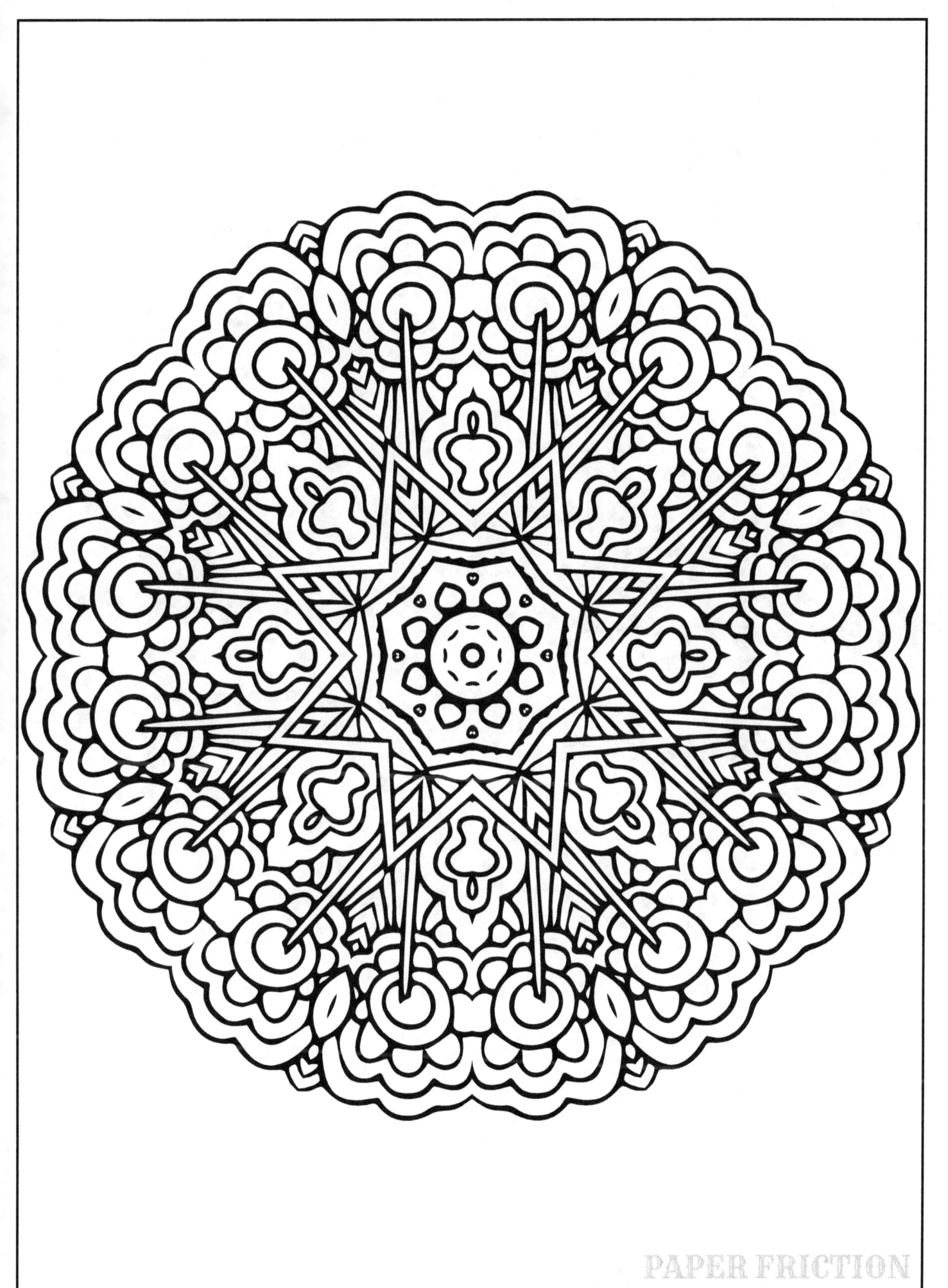

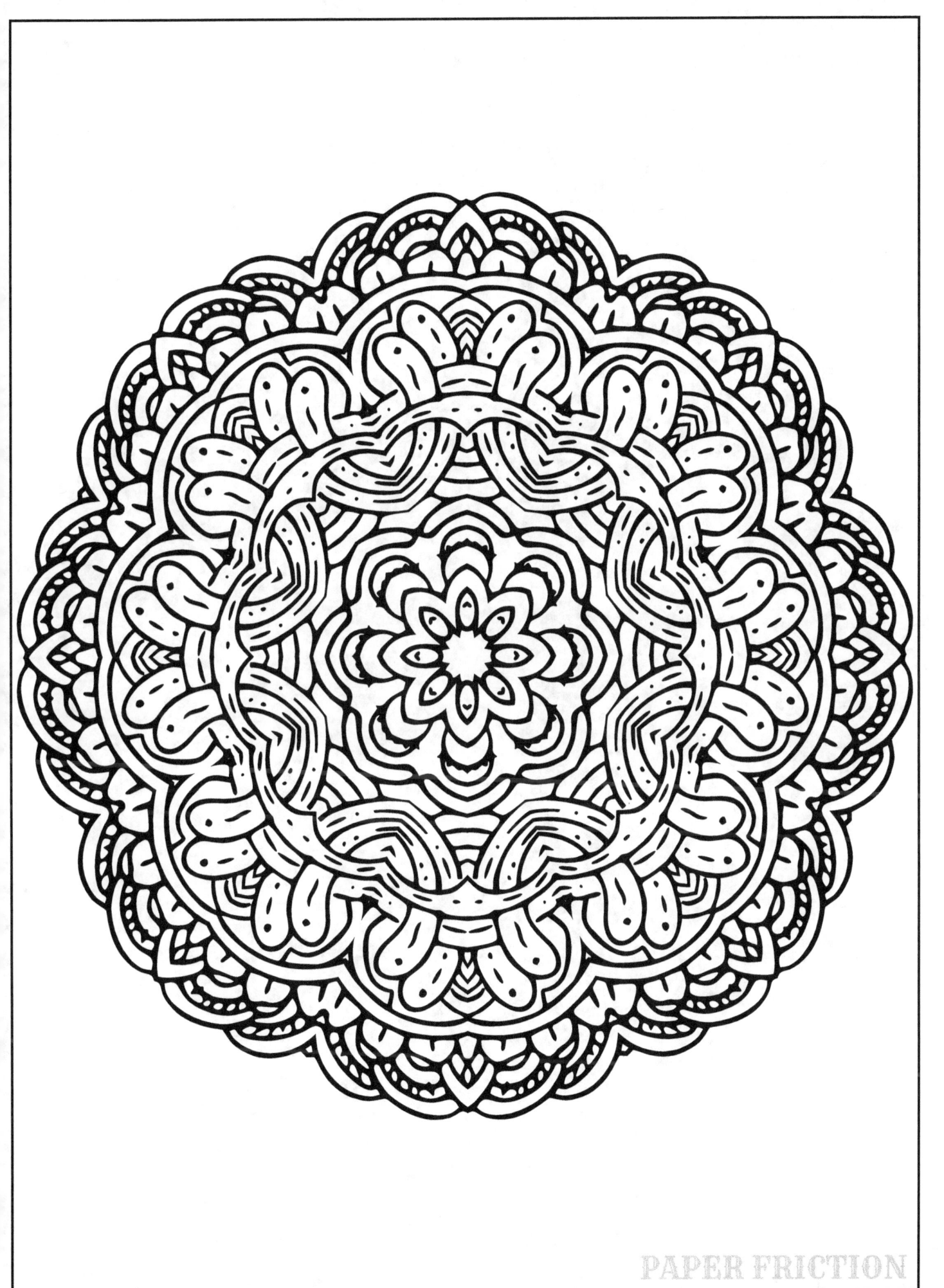

www.ingramcontent.com/pod-product-compliance
Lightning Source LLC
Chambersburg PA
CBHW060428220526
45465CB00008B/3051